Australian Industrial Relations in the 1980s

Australian Industrial Relations in the 1980s

Braham Dabscheck

OXFORD
UNIVERSITY PRESS

Melbourne
Oxford   Auckland   New York

OXFORD UNIVERSITY PRESS AUSTRALIA

Oxford   New York   Toronto
Delhi   Bombay   Calcutta   Madras   Karachi
Petaling Jaya   Singapore   Hong Kong   Tokyo
Nairobi,   Dar es Salaam   Cape Town
Melbourne   Auckland
and associated companies in
Berlin   Ibadan

OXFORD is a trade mark of Oxford University Press

National Library of Australia
Cataloguing-in-Publication data:

Dabscheck, Braham.
   Australian industrial relations in the 1980s.

   Bibliography.
   Includes index.
   ISBN 0 19 554921 X.

   1. Industrial relations—Australia. I. Title.
331'.0994

Edited by Merril Shead
Typeset by Setrite Typesetters Ltd
Printed by Impact Printing Pty Ltd
Published by Oxford University Press,
253 Normanby Road, South Melbourne, Australia

Contents

To Ben

Tables

Acknowledgements

I would like to express thanks to two people who have helped me in the preparation of this book: first, Kathy Cheeseman, who managed to decipher my script and to type with dedication and good humour; second, Pam Bedwell, for her encouragement and moral support during the project.

Braham Dabscheck
February 1988

Introduction

The major fascination of industrial relations is the clash of ideas about the world of work. Various individuals, groups, and organizations involved in, or with an interest in, industrial relations have different views and approaches concerning the best or most desirable way in which work relations should be conducted. It is the clash or battle between competing ideologies that constitutes the intellectual core of industrial relations.

New students invariably, it seems, expect industrial relations to be an interesting and exciting area of inquiry, because of the drama associated with the competing and different views that are so much a feature of real-world industrial relations. Such expectations are, however, usually dissipated once students begin ploughing through reading guides. There are three major reasons for this.

First, textbooks — on Australian industrial relations at least — tend to focus on description and to present extensive, detailed information on the various institutions that comprise the Australian industrial relations system. Second, there is the problem of the ubiquitous case study and/or the unquenchable appetite for the collection of mountains of facts. Most Australian researchers seem to devote themselves to fact grubbing, producing narrowly defined tracts that meticulously examine industry X, or union Y, or arbitration case Z, eschewing any attempt to delve into the more intellectually interesting and exciting theoretical issues associated with the clash of ideas that pervade real-world industrial relations. Third, apparently new ideas and issues seem continually to burst from the Australian industrial relations agenda. Partly as a result of the need to be up to date, and partly as a result of the addiction to collecting facts, industrial relations scribblers focus most of their attention on the quick fix of the here and now. While a case can be made for such writings, the major drawback of focusing on the here and now is being unaware of (similar) developments that have occurred in the past, and losing, or rather having no perspective on, the broader themes or rhythms that characterize Australian industrial relations.

The 1980s has been a decade of continuous change for Australian industrial relations. New and different approaches to industrial relations regulation have been experimented with, and different groups and organizations have vigorously competed with each other, on some occasions quite vociferously, in offering different solutions to what they perceive as the problems of the moment. At the macro level of Australian industrial relations, the 1980s have so far witnessed (the decade, at the time of writing, still has two years to go!) wage indexation; decentralized wage determination; a wages freeze; the Accord Mark I; two summits; the Hancock Report on industrial relations reform; the Accord Mark II; the emergence of the New Right; the introduction of a two-tiered wage determination system; the aborted 1987 Industrial Relations Bill; *Australia Reconstructed*, the Australian Council of Trade Unions (ACTU) and Trade Development Council (TDC) blueprint for the future; and various proposals for reform of the Australian Constitution.

This book is concerned with providing a critical and analytical (not to say, provocative) commentary on these developments. The orientation and major focus of the book presents and examines differing and competing ideas associated with these changes. In focusing on macro-level changes, issues such as affirmative action, non-discrimination, occupational health and safety, industrial democracy, technological change, and redundancy have not been addressed, because of space limitations only, not because they lack significance.

The book is organized as follows. Chapter 1 presents a survey of the major theoretical approaches that exist in industrial relations. The survey highlights the major ideas which pervade academic industrial relations and provides an intellectual backdrop for the material in subsequent chapters.

Chapter 2 examines the early 1980s: the centralized system of wage determination based on wage indexation, the breakdown of wage indexation in 1981, and decentralized wage determination in 1981 and 1982. Chapter 2 closes with a discussion of the Fraser Liberal–National Party coalition government's wages freeze and the freeze's implications for the Australian Conciliation and Arbitration Commission.

The 'consensus' policies critical to the election of the Hawke Labor government in March 1983 are presented in Chapter 3. The chapter examines the Australian Labor Party/ACTU Accord, the National Economic Summit Conference, and the subsequent introduction of a second system of wage indexation. The chapter concludes with a critique of the central tenets of wage indexation.

Chapter 4 focuses on the issue of industrial relations reform, which forced its way onto the industrial relations agenda in the period 1983–85. The chapter begins with a discussion of the meaning of reform and concludes with a critical examination of the Hancock Report, handed down in April 1985.

Chapter 5 examines the limits of consensus, or corporatist, approaches to industrial relations regulation. The unsuccessful July 1985 National Taxation Summit is the starting point, followed by examination of the economic, particularly balance of payments, problems experienced in 1985 and 1986, negotiation of the Accord Mark II, the subsequent national wage cases, which pointed to the demise of the second wage indexation experiment, and the eventual introduction of a two-tiered system of wage determination.

The second half of the 1980s witnessed the emergence of a group advocating that management should adopt a more aggressive or militant approach in dealing with unions and industrial tribunals. Many of the ideas of the New Right, as they have been called, have been asociated with the H. R. Nicholls Society Chapter 6 identifies reasons for the emergence of the New Right and critically examines their ideas.

Chapter 7 examines recent developments. The rise and fall of the 1987 Industrial Relations Bill, the ACTU−TDC plan for Australia's future, in *Australia Reconstructed*, and changes to the Australian Constitution recommended by a constitutional commission are closely scrutinized.

Chapter 8 recaps and pulls together the book's major themes and ideas.

CHAPTER 1

Of Mountains and Routes Over Them:
A Survey of Theories of Industrial Relations

A number of competing theories have developed over the years in the attempt to deal with real-world industrial relations. Five major theoretical approaches, and some variants of them — namely Dunlop's systems model, pluralism, Marxism, corporatism, and theories of regulation — are compared and contrasted in this chapter. In examining these theories, attention will be directed to three key issues: first, the notion of the public interest — whether the respective theories incorporate such a notion, or use an alternative analytical device to explain the nature of the interaction(s) that characterize(s) industrial relations; second, the nature and role of the state, in particular whether the state is viewed as an independent or dependent variable; third, the level of analysis, that is whether the theory is aggregated or disaggregated and/or whether it is societal based or firm based.

Subsequent chapters demonstrate that the various approaches to industrial relations regulation which have been experimented with or advocated in Australia in the 1980s derive their intellectual inspiration, even if unwittingly, from the theories examined in this chapter. For example, calls to deregulate the labour market derive from theories of regulation; proposals to encourage or enhance industrial relations at the firm or enterprise level stem from firm-based pluralist models; the Accord and centralized systems of wage determination such as wage indexation are antipodean applications of corporatism; and calls for a decentralized approach to industrial relations (as distrinct from a deregulated one) are based on societal models of pluralism.

DUNLOP'S SYSTEMS APPROACH

Dunlop defined an industrial relations system as consisting

of three groups of actors — workers and their organizations, managers and their organizations, and governmental agencies concerned with the work community. These groups interact within a specified environment comprised of three interrelated contexts: the technology, the market or budgetary constraints, and the power relations in the larger community and the derived status of the actors. An industrial relations system creates an ideology or a commonly shared body of ideas and beliefs regarding the interaction and roles of the actors which helps to bind the system together (Dunlop, 1958, p. 383).

He also argued that

The establishment of ... procedures and rules ... is the centre of attention of an industrial relations system ... the establishment and administration of these rules is the major concern or output of the industrial relations sub-system of industrial society (Dunlop, 1958, p. 13).

While this approach is strong on structure, it tells us little about processes and the motivation of the actors. To breathe some life into Dunlop it is necessary to assume that the actors are desirous of achieving their respective goals. Also, as Margerison has pointed out, Dunlop's definition of industrial relations, with its concentration on rules and rule making,

tends to ignore the essential element of all industrial relations, that of the nature and development of conflict itself ... industrial relations [according to Dunlop] ... is more concerned with studying the resolution of industrial conflict than with its generation (Margerison, 1969, p. 273).

Dunlop is therefore exposed to the charge that the systems model is a conservative tool designed to ensure the maintenance of the status quo. Criticism has also been directed at Dunlop's treatment of 'actors' — more than three distinct actors can interact within an industrial relations system.

Dunlop is silent, or at best ambiguous, on the issue of the public interest. His notion of a common ideology shared by the actors, and his focus on rules and rule making, may imply that the absence of either would not enhance the attainment of the public interest. He does, however, contemplate the possibility of an industrial relations system without a common ideology:

> In a community in which the managers hold a highly paternalistic view toward workers and the workers hold there is no function for managers, there would be no common ideology in which each actor provided a legitimate role for the other; the relationship within such a work community would be regarded as volatile, and no stability would [be] likely to be achieved in the industrial relations system (Dunlop, 1958, p. 17).

The role of the state is poorly developed in Dunlop's model. He employs the term *governmental agencies* to incorporate the role of the state. However, the state's involvement within an industrial relations system is more complex than this. Dunlop's analysis excludes the role of government(s) and the various superior courts which supervise the operation of industrial relations governmental agencies. Dunlop could deflect this criticism by claiming that the various organs of the state pursue a common and unified objective. It is equally if not more likely, however, that they could be pulling and pushing in different directions. In Australia, for example, there is a need to distinguish state and federal governments, and superior courts make decisions which both define and restrict the powers available to unions and employers as well as the various organs of the state.

Dunlop is also ambiguous about the dependency or independency of governmental agencies. Presumably, in Dunlop's view, such agencies aid the other two actors as they interact. It is unclear, however, whether these agencies follow the bidding of the parties, or are directed by an external body (such as government), or develop their own approach to issues which confront them.

Dunlop focuses his analysis on the internal operation of a representative industrial relations system. Implicit in his approach is the notion that each system is unique, its form and evolution being determined by its own set of external constraints. Dunlop, then, assumes that there are no interconnections between industrial relations systems; to do otherwise would complicate his model and open up the possibility of having to analyse the actions and strategies of numerous actors. It is conceivable, however, that in seeking to arrive at an adequate understanding of industrial relations within a particular nation state, the inter-dependency, or the nature of the relationship, that exists between different industrial relations (sub)systems may be equally if not more crucial than that which occurs within respective industrial relations (sub)systems.

Kochan, McKersie, and Cappelli (1984) have attempted to develop a theory of industrial relations which explicitly takes account of or acknowledges the interdependencies that exist between different industrial relations (sub)systems; interestingly they have undertaken such a task using systems theory. Their work developed as a theoretical response to the emergence of the aggressive anti-unionism of militant management which has occurred in the United States over the last decade or so. In responding theoretically to the emergence of this American New Right, Kochan *et al.* have suggested two modifications to systems theory: first, to introduce the notion of strategic choice to decision making; second, to identify different locations (or levels) at which strategic choices, or more correctly industrial relations, may occur. They distinguish between three different locations. First are 'those associated with workers as individuals or work groups and their relations with the immediate work environment'. Second are 'the familiar ones associated with the practice of collective bargaining and the implementation of personnel policy'. Third is the 'global level', which may involve tripartite (corporatist?), national-level negotiations between government, unions and employer associations, and

> where unions are pressing for a more meaningful role in decisions regarding investment, union recognition, introduction of new technology, controls over outsourcing or subcontracting and the design of work organization systems in new plants ... government policies toward union organizing ... [and] business decisions ... [concerning] which markets to pursue, where to locate plants, and whether to make or buy components (Kochan *et al.*, 1984, pp. 22–3).

Several comments can be made about their model. First, while it is undoubtedly correct that the various independent organizations involved in industrial relations (let alone other areas of social activity) make strategic choices, the idea of strategic choices begs the question of why or for what reasons strategic choices are made? Kochan *et al.* have focused on the *means* of decision making rather than the *ends*, or goals, of such decisions. The question they need to address is, What goals or objectives are those involved in industrial relations desirous of achieving as they make their respective strategic choices?

Second, it is unclear why Kochan *et al.* have attempted to develop their new or alternative model within the tradition of Dunlop's systems approach. Systems theory is based on the assumption that industrial relations actors share an ideology. Kochan *et al.* are attempting to develop a model based on aggressive anti-unionism, an explicit-conflict situation, where management/capital is seeking to destroy unions. This is the antithesis of shared ideology. To be fair, Kochan *et al.* (1984, p. 20) are aware of this. With such disparity between Dunlop's systems model and the real world, would it not be advisable to experiment with and develop completely different or alternative models?

Third, Kochan, McKersie, and Cappelli's use of the concept *location* poses additional theoretical problems for Dunlop's systems model. It should be remembered that Dunlop defined an industrial relations system as consisting of three actors. In fact he was very explicit, if not dogmatic, on this point, stating that 'every industrial relations system involves three groups of actors' (Dunlop, 1958, p. viii). In developing the idea of locations at which industrial relations can occur Kochan *et al.* implicitly increase the potential number of actors participating in industrial relations: different actors at different locations implies increasing numbers of actors. As the number of actors increases, the various ways in which they may combine and interact also increase. It is not inconceivable that different sets of actors will enter into coalitions with each other (either within or across their respective positions in the authority structure) to achieve their goals and objectives at the expense of other (coalitions of ?) actors.

It should also be remembered that their third location — the global level — incorporates the role of government (and potentially other organs of the state) and finance capital. To the extent that government (or the state) becomes a key actor in its own right it would follow that for both theoretical and empirical reasons it would be necessary to conceive of industrial relations in (global) societal terms. To state this proposition in an alternative form: if the implication of Kochan, McKersie, and Cappelli's ideas concerning location is that we need to relate the whole (the global nature of industrial relations) to any particular part (locations one or two) to be able to comprehend and understand what is occurring in that part, it follows that there is a need to develop models of industrial relations based on the whole.

PLURALISM

Many disciplines within the social sciences, other than industrial relations — philosophy, anthropology, sociology, and political science — have developed theoretical approaches to analyse different phenomena, which they have respectively described as *pluralism*. So varied and diverse are the notions of pluralism within the social sciences that it might be more appropriate to refer to what Hyman describes as 'pluralism's pluralism' (Hyman, 1978, p. 177). This section will not attempt the daunting task of surveying the intellectual roots, the evolution, and the nuances of pluralism within different disciplines,[1] but it will examine the North American political science model of pluralism, developed in the 1950s, to provide a reference for the subsequent examination of industrial relations pluralism.

North American political science pluralism of the 1950s represents a model of political decision making depicting the interaction that occurs between and among private interest groups and the various organs of the state. The political process is viewed as being open and fluid, 'essentially a twofold process involving competition among political elites and bargaining among interest groups' (Kelso, 1978, p. 13). With this model, power is dispersed among a large number of varied and diverse interest groups. No single interest group or elite is able to become dominant because of the countervailing power of other interest groups and elites. Or, as Connolly says:

Pluralism ... portrays the system as a balance of power among overlapping economic, religious, ethnic, and geographical groupings.

Each 'group' has some voice in shaping socially binding decisions; each constrains and is constrained through the process of mutual group adjustments; and all major groups share a broad system of beliefs and values which encourages conflict to proceed within established channels and allows initial disagreement to dissolve into compromise solutions (Connolly, 1969, p. 3).

The political system, then, is regarded as one of checks and balances, a self-regulating mechanism where interest groups, in pursuing self-interest, restrain each other. It is akin to the economist's market-place where political entrepreneurs compete with each other for political favours in furthering the objectives of their respective organizations.

Within this model the concept of the public interest operates at two distinct levels. At the first level it is seen to be important that the system should continue to operate. Superficially, political science pluralism may appear to be a static model designed to ensure the maintenance of the status quo. The model, however, is concerned with understanding the process of political change — of explaining how the system moves from one position of balance or equilibrium to another. Change is viewed as occurring incrementally or discretely, rather than in big chunks or in a revolutionary manner, and results from the incessant interaction of numerous and varied interest groups. Furthermore, to talk of balance or equilibrium is not to imply that there is an equality of power between interest groups. It is recognized that there will be differences in the distribution of power at different points in time; no single interest group, however, will be able to dominate all other interest groups.

At the second level, when references are made to the public interest it should be viewed simply as a tactical device employed by interest groups to assure respectability for naked self-interest. As Barkin argues:

Absolutely no public has its own static interest any more than an absolute reality with unvarying truth exists. Publics are ways of conceiving activities, and interests are means of indicating the value assigned to them by their participants and others. No such thing as *the* public activity, *the* society, or *the* public interest exists. The public interest as such, the claim of a specific group that its interests should be recognized and shared by all other groups, is a myth (Barkin, 1971, p. 96).

Political science pluralism is ambiguous on the role of the state. The arena model views the state as the locus in which interest groups jockey with each other for their respective places in the political sun. The state is dependent in the sense that interest groups capture the state, or rather the appropriate part of the state, to enhance the pursuit of their organizational goals. The umpire model, on the other hand, regards the state as independent. It not only establishes the rules of interaction and adjudicates disputes, but also initiates action to ensure that any interest group which becomes too powerful is brought back to the fold. (Presumably if the state becomes too powerful, private interest groups initiate action which will restrain its activities.) Alternatively, the umpire model can be watered down to include the various organs of the state as an additional set of interest groups involved in the exchanges that occur within a pluralistic society.

Political science pluralism employs a disaggregated societal-based model that posits that the political system consists of a multitude of small, disconnected parts or subsectors. Interest groups organize themselves and marshal resources at those parts of the system that are of relevance to them, and by definition ignore those parts that are seen as irrelevant. The model assumes that the links between the various parts or subsectors of the system are limited and weak.

The major criticism of political science pluralism is that while it may usefully analyse the nature of the interaction that occurs between established groups, it ignores and/or downplays the existence of new groups that find it difficult to gain access to the mainstream of political life. It is also criticized as a distortion of social reality and for being essentially conservative. Wolff, for example, argues that

> pluralist theory functions ideologically by tending to deny new groups or interests access to the political plateau. It does this by ignoring their existence in practice, not by denying their claim in theory. The result is that pluralism has a breaking effect on social change; it slows down transformation in the system of group adjustment but does not set up an absolute barrier to change (Wolff, 1969, p. 54).

The political science model of pluralism, with its focus on a large number of groups pursuing self-interest in a disaggregated manner (i.e. at that part of the system where concessions are forthcoming), would appear to have a natural affinity with the world of industrial relations, where interactions between different unions, employers, and organs of the state also occur in a disaggregated manner. With industrial relations, of course, the parties do not confine the pursuit of self-interest to the polity, but also have access to what might be called the economist's market-place. The advantage of explicitly incorporating the market into the analysis is that it helps to overcome the problem of the denial of access to new groups, which is a weakness of political science pluralism. The market, or rather change in the market, has the potential to provide new interest groups with increased benefits and concomitant prestige, notwithstanding their inability to gain access to the cartel that dominates the political process. As new industries and sectors rise (and old ones fall), as respective organizations increase (decrease) their effectiveness in the market-place, they simultaneously bring about a new balance that enshrines their enhanced (reduced) position. The market would become an additional variable which would reflect changes in the relative positions of the various interest groups regarded as constituting a pluralistic industrial relations system.

A major problem, however, with applying political science pluralism to industrial relations is its ambivalence with regard to the role of the state. This could possibly be rectified by assuming that the various organs of the state are independent organizations pursuing unique objectives; the various organs of the state could be simply viewed as just another set of institutions operating within the framework of a pluralistic industrial relations system.

With a few modifications, then, political science pluralism might have been adapted to the world of industrial relations. However, the model that was subsequently developed had little connection with the North American political science model.[2]

Industrial relations pluralism[3] is essentially a British phenomenon and is generally linked to the ferment of ideas associated with the Donovan Report (1968) into British industrial relations in the second half of the 1960s. Possibly the clearest exposition is provided by Fox (1966, 1973, 1974, 1979), although in his hands its ultimate function was that of a straw man.[4] Fox argues that the firm should be viewed in plural terms:

the enterprise is a coalition of individuals and groups with their own aspirations and perceptions which they naturally see as valid and which they seek to express in action if such is required ... individuals and groups with widely varying priorities agree to collaborate in social structures which enable all participants to get something of what they want; the terms of collaboration being settled by bargaining (Fox, 1974, pp. 260–1).

Fox also assumes that there is 'something approximating a balance of power' between the parties and that they pursue a policy of mutual survival (Fox, 1974, pp. 263, 265). He is uncertain, however, about how to regard the role of conflict:

A certain amount of overt conflict and disputation is welcomed as evidence that not all aspirations are being either sapped by hopelessness or suppressed by power. On the other hand, conflict above a certain level is felt to be evidence that the ground rules need changing; that marginal adjustments in rewards or work rules are required; that management is failing in some way to find the appropriate compromise or synthesis (Fox, 1974, p. 262).

He is wary of the possibility that the parties may pursue claims which could lead to the breakdown of pluralistic consensus:

It would obviously be possible for one party to make claims which the other found totally unacceptable and on which compromise or synthesis proved impossible. The pluralist presumption would be that in such a case the consensual ethic governing joint regulation would be ruptured, and a forced collaboration would emerge when one party succeeded in coercing the other. The operation of a pluralistic system requires that such situations should be the exception rather than the rule, and that in the main the claims of each party fall within the range found bearable by the other (Fox, 1974, pp. 264–5).

Some comparisons can be drawn between Fox's model of industrial relations pluralism and that of North American political science. Fox's analysis is couched at the level of the firm, whereas the political science model is societal. Hence Fox's analysis is restricted to a small number of interest groups, whereas political science pluralism incorporates hordes of interest groups. Directing attention to this difference in numbers may appear to be carping.

However, it does expose Fox's analysis to some important questioning. Political science pluralism does not require equality of power to exist between the numerous interest groups. It is recognized that at any point in time, inequalities in the balance of power can exist. The model maintains, however, that no single interest group will be able to dominate all other interest groups. An interest group that increases its power will be dragged back to the fold by the actions of other interest groups — the notion of checks and balances. With Fox's model, on the other hand, there are only a small number of interest groups — basically workers/unions and employers/capital — and it is necessary to postulate an equality of power. To not do so would imply that one interest group dominates the other, which by definition destroys the plural-firm assumption.

Fox's firm-based model eschews interest groups going outside the firm — for example, making use of politics — in seeking to achieve their goals. The political science model, on the other hand, is explicitly concerned with the interaction of interest groups as political animals. There are problems in Fox having adopted a narrow, firm-based approach: not only does he ignore the reality — and, it could be argued, much of the richness of real-world industrial relations — but also, and most significantly, he has no way of incorporating the role of the state into his analysis. Given Fox's concern with the continuation of bargaining, with tolerable levels of industrial conflict, and with mutual survival, it can possibly be assumed that the state can intervene under the public-interest rubric. Dunlop's systems model is stronger on the role of the state than is Fox's model of industrial relations pluralism.

Interestingly Fox is one of the strongest critics of industrial relations pluralism.[5] He argues

that industrial society, while manifestly on one level a congeries of small special interest groups vying for scarce goods, status, or influence, is more fundamentally characterized in terms of the overarching exploitation of one class by another, of the propertyless by the propertied, of the less by the more powerful. From this view, any talk of 'checks and balances', however apt for describing certain subsidary phenomena simply confuses our understanding of the primary dynamics which shape and move society — a useful confusion indeed for the major power holders since it obscures the domination of society by its ruling strata through institutions and assumptions which operate to exclude anything approaching a genuine power balance (Fox, 1974, p. 274).

The industrial relations pluralist model, then, is seen as a distortion of reality, a confidence trick designed to maintain and legitimize the status quo. There is a degree of confusion, however, associated with Fox's analysis. First, in criticizing industrial relations pluralism he has switched his level of analysis away from the firm to society as a whole, away from special-interest groups to classes ('strata'?). Some explanation of the reasons for and implications of such switching should have been provided. Second, and notwithstanding the foregoing, he appears to be generalizing his firm-based model across society as a whole, introducing a new set of theoretical problems.

We will follow Fox and assume the existence of a large number of firms of the type that he has described. However, an additional assumption will be incorporated — namely that the firms compete with each other. Fox's model will thus be broadened, merely, to incorporate the external world in which the firm operates (and to move away from the firm machinations). This approach has a number of interesting implications. First, while there may be inequalities of power within firms, it needs to be established that all firms will be characterized by the same distribution of power *between* interest groups/classes *within* the firm. It is conceivable, if not highly likely, that the relative distribution of subservience and domination will vary between firms. Second, there could be disparities in the distribution of power or dominance *between* as distinct from *within* firms. Strong or prosperous firms, and the interest groups/classes contained therein, may enjoy an abundance of economic and social rewards vis-à-vis weaker firms and the respective interest groups/classes contained therein[6] — as well as the unemployed. Third, there is the possibility that different firms will form coalitions with each other to restrain the activities of other firms. Fourth, coalitions may be formed by different interest groups/classes within firms to restrain the activities of other (coalitions of) interest groups/classes. Two subtypes could be distinguished: first, where interest groups/classes from the same authority position within firms combine; second, where interest groups/classes from different authority positions within the respective firms combine to counter the activities of other firms and/or coalitions of interest groups/classes.

Fox's second line of attack was to argue, in an influential article co-authored with Flanders, that British industrial relations was subject to what Durkheim would describe as a condition of anomie — 'a state of normlessness resulting from a breakdown in social regulation' (Fox and Flanders, 1969, p. 156). They went on to identify four sources of disorder in British industrial relations:

1 situations in which one group, against the resistance of another, seeks to change the procedural norms and nature of the system;
2 a similar situation with respect to the system's substantive norms; the degree of tension between the prevailing norms and the aspirations of one or more relevant groups has become so great that it provokes challenge and conflict;
3 an absence of regulation about certain issues on which one group at least has normative aspirations . . . problem situations come under *ad hoc*, piecemeal solutions, often arrived at only after conflict between opposing groups who have brought their divergent interests and values to bear upon the particular case. Until agreement has been reached on the need for regulation, however, the prospect of recurrent disorder persists;
4 when these second and third sources of disorder multiply, their very frequency and extent may, in appropriate circumstances, create . . . a progressive fragmentation and breakdown of existing regulative systems (Fox and Flanders, 1969, p. 161).

Two criticisms of this analysis can be made. First, and side-stepping the question of whether they have interpreted Durkheim's notion of anomie appropriately,[7] they appear to have confused change with anomie. It is extremely difficult to believe that they could be surprised that the interest groups/classes/actors in industrial relations will make substantive claims that either side does not regard as being unreasonable (factor two), will differ over the procedural ways in which conflict should be regulated (factors one and four), or will bring new items to the bargaining table (factor three). All are part and parcel of industrial relations systems in Western capitalist countries. Furthermore, given their sociological backgrounds it is difficult to comprehend why Fox and Flanders eschew and denigrate the role of conflict. Political science pluralism, for example, would have little difficulty in accommodating the issues they raise. It would predict that the various interest groups operating in industrial relations would make both substantive and procedural bids and bring new issues to the bargaining table, and that through such interactions a new balance or equilibrium would be achieved.

Second, Fox and Flanders fail to appreciate that those who have benefited from the changes that have occurred — Goldthorpe (1977, pp. 191−202), for example, identified the gains achieved by workers at the shopfloor in the 1960s — would experience some difficulty in being convinced by 'wise' men from universities that the system was in fact anomic.

MARXISM

Relative to industrial relations, Marxist theory is problematical. First, Marxism in the social sciences, as distinct from industrial relations, is dynamic, fluid, and characterized by major and at times bitter debates. Taylor (1982) pointed to the existence of numerous variations within Marxism and radical sociology. Significantly he found it easier to urge others to adopt an avowedly Marxist approach to the study of industrial relations than to develop and/or apply his own approach. Second, Marxists regard it as inappropriate to abstract the study of industrial relations from the totality of social phenomena. Industrial relations is too narrow a focus to be worthy of separate study. Third, and as a result of the foregoing, Marxism is relatively underdeveloped within industrial relations.

Hyman has probably devoted more time than any other writer to the development of a distinctly Marxist approach to industrial relations.[8] He has identified two key assumptions of the approach:

The first is that capitalist social relations of production reflect and reproduce a structured antagonism of interests between capital and labour. The second is that capitalism simultaneously organizes workers collectively (since the capitalist labour process is essentially collective in character), and hence generates the material basis for effective resistance to capital and the priorities of the capitalist mode of production. What is conventionally studied as industrial relations may then be conceived as a fetishized presentation of the class struggle and the various forms in which it is (at least temporarily) constrained, fragmented and routinized (Hyman, 1980, p. 42).

Whereas the systems approach refers to actors, and pluralism to interest groups, Marxists are concerned with classes. Hyman argues that between the capitalist class and the working class 'there exists a radical conflict of interests, which underlies everything that occurs in industrial relations' (Hyman, 1975, p. 23).

While the positioning of classes may be determined by the capitalist mode of production, it is unclear whether Marxist analysis in industrial relations is firm based or society based. One approach has been to focus analysis on the labour process at the firm level. Furthermore, attention is directed at the process of technological change and the concomitant division of labour, which separates and divides the working class, reducing and weakening their ability to combine as a class and usher in revolutionary change (Collins, 1978). Alternatively, the analysis of class relations is generalized from the firm to society as a whole. All sections of the working class are seen as having interests in common which unite them in an all-encompassing struggle with all sections of (united) capital.

However, in generalizing from the firm to society Marxism runs into the same problems as Fox's model of pluralism (and Dunlop's systems model). The distribution of power between classes/interest groups in different firms will manifest itself in different ways, and conflict between firms, rather than within firms, may be more significant for gaining an understanding of the workings of capitalism.[9] This generalized, society-based Marxist model, in postulating the existence of class conflict, is built on the assumption of coalition formation, and it is specific on the issue of formation of coalitions. Coalitions will only be formed by classes/interest groups from the same authority position within respective firms: workers form coalitions with workers, capital with capital. It ignores the possibility of coalition formation by firms, or by classes/interest groups across authority positions: workers and capital in firm *A* may combine with capital in firm *B* to restrain the activities of workers in firm *B*, and/or combine against workers and capital in firm *C*.

Criticism can also be directed at the proposition that class conflict is essentially revolutionary; it needs to be established that the conflict which separates classes is of an explosive type which will bring about revolutionary change.[10] It is conceivable that classes will be able to regulate the conflict that divides them, and via negotiations slowly and less dramatically bring about change (Dahrendorf, 1959, pp. 124−36).

Furthermore, unions, in pursuing the interests of workers, have generally speaking sought here-and-now economic improvements rather than embarking on a course of revolutionary change. Marxists could contend that unions and their members are subject to false consciousness and could advocate the need to replace union leaders with intellectuals from the revolutionary party who will lead unions to their appointed (Leninist) destiny. However, this in turn raises the vexed issue of what is *true* consciousness (the knowing of something that may not exist in the real world), and the possibility that both the membership and home-grown leaders of unions might reject the 'social mysticism' of intellectuals who emerge from outside the economic struggle.[11] Additionally, as Crouch has argued:

As soon as workers acquire some power, capital makes concessions to them; and given workers' incremental approach, they take the concessions, with the result that the pattern of demands and gains follows the contours of the concessions which capital is able and willing to make — not that of the points which might overthrow capitalism (Crouch, 1982, p. 131).

Our earlier examination of the systems approach and pluralism revealed that the role of the state was inadequately developed. Marxism, in comparison, has a well-developed stance.[12] As Engels asserted, 'the executive of the modern State is but a committee for managing the common affairs of the whole bourgeoisie' (Hyman, 1975, p. 121).

Two problems with this approach can be identified. First, the state can and does make concessions to workers and unions. The usual response of Marxists, such as Hyman, is to describe this as a policy of incorporation which has the intention 'of integrating the working class into capitalist society, thus serving as a mechanism of social control' (Hyman, 1975, p. 143); the state is prepared to grant short-term concessions to unions and workers as a means of ensuring long-term dominance and control. However, this response runs into some serious problems. First, how long is the long term and what is the use of such a notion if the long term is defined as consisting of a stream of short terms? Second, is social change something that occurs in a grand and spectacular fashion at certain allotted points in time, or is it a gradual process occurring on a gradual incremental basis? If the answer to this question is yes, social reality is more consistent with the predictions of political science pluralism than it is with Marxism.

The second problem is that capital is not homogeneous — it comprises competing factions and fractions (Strinati, 1982). The implication of this is that a concession gained from the state by one fraction of capital may impose additional costs and burdens and/or may have been at the expense of other fractions of capital. For example, increased tariffs may provide aid to that fraction of capital (and the workers employed therein) which competes with overseas producers, and simultaneously may increase the cost of inputs to other fractions of capital (imposing costs on other workers), who are thus forced to purchase the commodity or commodities at a higher price. What determines the distribution of state largess between different fractions of capital? One answer could be that the most powerful fractions of capital are most successful in acquiring concessions from the state. The problem with this answer, however, is that the state, as evidenced in Australia, in fact provides aid and protection to struggling and declining industries, with old and outdated capital/machinery, to the vexation of the high-productivity resource-based industries. Furthermore, it is conceivable that the state itself may play an important part in determining which of the competing claims of the fractions of capital (interest groups) will receive aid and protection.

CORPORATISM

The use of wages and incomes policies in Britain and Western Europe during the 1960s and 1970s was accompanied by the development of a theoretical literature described as *corporatism*.

Its major theoretical innovation is that it regards the state, in its relations with the other institutions which constitute society, as being autonomous and independent. In the words of Anderson 'the state is no longer the passive recipient of group pressures, but an autonomous force in the political equation' (1977, p. 129).

There is debate within the literature as to whether corporatism should be viewed as 'a political structure' (Panitch 1977, p. 66), 'an economic system' (Winkler, 1976, p. 103), 'a system of interest representation' (Schmitter, 1974, p. 13), or 'an institutional pattern of policy formation' (Lehmbruch, 1977, p. 94). Crouch defines corporatism as

a system of politico-economic organisation ... The economy remains capitalist in the sense of being privately owned, but the stability of the system is ensured through the close *integration* of political, economic and moral forces, rather than through their separation. And workers (and others) are subordinated, not through individualism, but through the very fact of belonging to collectivities, organizations; the organizations which represent them also regulate them (Crouch, 1979a, pp. 123–4).

In a corporatist world the state directly intervenes in the operation of the political and economic system under the banner of the public interest.[13] Society, it is argued, cannot afford the luxury of competition and conflict between the various organizations which constitute society. Conflict and competition must be replaced by co-operation and consensus in pursuit of the common good. The state directly intervenes to bring about an end to conflict and to lead the way down the path of national progress. Corporatism requires organizations to put aside sectional interests and concentrate on the so-called 'needs of the nation as a whole'. The state interprets and defines these needs and incorporates and harnesses the activities of organizations in pursuing the common good. The state and the representatives of capital and labour interact and make decisions for the good of all. The responsibility of the representatives of labour and capital is not only to educate their respective constituents as to the wisdom of the decisions reached, but also to act as agents of control to ensure that the decisions reached are observed and enforced.

The literature offers models of corporatism. Schmitter, for example, contrasts societal and state corporatism, whereas Lehmbruch distinguishes between liberal and authoritarian corporatism; whether control comes from above or below constitutes the dividing line. With societal (liberal) corporatism, control is exercised from below and reduces the independence of the state in that 'the legitimacy and functioning of the state ... [is] primarily or exclusively dependent on the ability of singular, non-competitive, hierarchically ordered representative "corporations" '. With state (authoritarian) corporatism the state is seen as being dominant, in that 'similarly structured "corporations" were created by and kept as auxiliary and dependent organs of the state which founded its legitimacy and effective functioning on other bases' (Schmitter, 1974, p. 20). The third model, developed by Crouch, is defined as 'bargained corporatism': the state bargains and negotiates with society's various, constituent organizations/interest groups.[14] The advantage of this model is that while it treats the state as an independent variable, it simultaneously acknowledges that the state cannot pursue its objectives in isolation from the actions and desires of the various institutions which constitute society. If the state is to achieve its goals, it will need to bargain, negotiate, and enter into compromises. In a sense Crouch's notion of bargained corporatism can be viewed as a special case of political science pluralism — an aggregated societal-based model that explicitly incorporates the state as a separate and independent entity.[15]

Two major criticisms have been directed at corporatism. The first concerns the assumption that there can be an end to conflict and that co-operation and consensus can be brought into being by an omnipotent state. It is conceivable that the various organizations which make up society may reject the interpretation of the public interest defined for them by the state. If they continue to assert self-interest, and in the absence of constraints on their activities, the corporate consensus desired by the state will quickly disintegrate. More fundamentally, conflict, notwithstanding attempts by the state to assume its existence away, is an ever-present feature of social life. Furthermore, the supposition that the state can enforce consensus is a contradiction in terms. If the state has to resort to force to induce recalcitrant organizations to observe 'consensus', it becomes an agent of repression and control and simultaneously destroys a key assumption upon which corporatism is based.

The second criticism concerns the level of analysis at which corporatism proceeds. Corporatism analyses society in terms of lumps or aggregates; it refers to the state, capital, and labour. It implies that all three are monolithic and that peak representative bodies can control and regulate their respective constituent parts. The relationship, however, between central union bodies and affiliates, and of individual unions to their rank and file members, is dynamic and complex. Central union bodies are not in a position to dictate to affiliates, and rank and file members will pursue claims directly with employers at the shopfloor level.[16] Similarly, the relationship between the various fractions of capital is dynamic and complex. The various fractions of capital are in continual competition — what is income to one is a cost to another. Furthermore, as has been mentioned earlier, the state is not a single uniform entity. Distinctions can be drawn between the government — or in a federal system, such as Australia's, governments — and the various courts, tribunals, and statutory bodies which regulate the affairs of the numerous institutions within society.

THEORIES OF REGULATION

Crouch claims that

> It is remarkable to what extent the recent spread of interest in the state has led to the elaboration of social theory solely within the Marxist tradition ..: It is particularly strange that so little has emerged from the American pluralist tradition of political science, which has for so long dominated the subject and prided itself on the superiority over Marxism of its ability to conceptualise the political (Crouch, 1979b, p. 13).

However, it is equally remarkable that someone as perceptive and diligent as Crouch has ignored the development of corporatism, to which he himself has made major contributions, and that he can be blind to a major intellectual innovation in North American social science during the 1970s — namely the development of theories of regulation. Theories of regulation are concerned with analysing the relationship between regulatory bodies and the economic agents or interest groups which they regulate. They combine contributions from political science, law, administration, and economics, and critically examine institutions which have been brought into being to regulate, among other things, airlines, railways, television, airwaves, utilities, occupational safety, health, and protection of the environment. Such theories can also be applied to institutions regulating the various interest groups in industrial relations. For Australian students the activities of industrial tribunals would seem to be an obvious area of interest.

Two competing models of regulation can be contrasted. The first is referred to as *capture theory*, where the government and regulatory bodies are viewed as passive instruments, merely used and manipulated by private interest groups. While the rhetoric of regulation is to protect the public from so-called breakdowns in the economic system, the reality is 'that, as a rule, regulation is acquired by the industry and is designed and operated primarily for its benefit' (Stigler, 1971, p. 3). In short, interest groups make use of the coercive power of the state to protect and advance self-interest.

Capture theory employs the conventional supply and demand framework of the economist to explain the phenomenon of law making. Laws are not made in a vacuum: they result from the interaction of politicians and interest groups. Politicians are viewed as being similar to entrepreneurs seeking to enhance their electoral success. They *supply* programmes and support legislation that enhances their ability to win votes and to raise finance to support their electoral campaigns. Interest groups *demand* programmes and legislation that protect and promote their interests. They are more aware of the costs and benefits of regulation and are better informed and more able to lobby politicians than the public at large. The benefits of regulation are concentrated, whereas the costs, which the general public incur, are diffused. Capture theory maintains that the superior organization and political effectiveness of interest groups ensure that regulation will serve their interests rather than those of the general public.

Two major criticisms can be levelled at capture theory.[17] The first concerns the assumption that regulators meekly do the bidding of interest groups. Capture theory may provide useful insights into the nature of the interaction between interest groups and the politician, but it fails to explain why regulators should be equally hapless and passive. Second, capture theory assumes that the interests of the regulated are uniform. What happens in situations where regulators are confronted by a number of well-organized interest groups whose interests are opposed? How do regulators arrive at a decision in such a situation? It is conceivable that regulators attempt to apply their own ideas to the problems associated with regulation.

The second model of regulation can be loosely described as a *bargaining theory*.[18] It assumes that the individuals who preside over regulatory bodies are independent and have their own notions of how the various problems associated with regulation can be resolved. Regulators interact with interest groups and seek to lead them down a desired path of regulation. The personnel of regulatory bodies are involved in a balancing act — an act which is, however, more complex than simply balancing the competing claims of interest groups. They balance the expectations of the parties with their interpretation of what the problems of regulation require.

Both are disaggregated societal-based models. Various interest groups focus attention and devote resources to that part of the body politic which is relevant to them, and interact with their own *unique* fraction of the state. Capture theory views the notion of the public interest as a smokescreen behind which interest groups seek to justify and rationalize the pursuit of self-interest. Bargaining theory is silent on the role of the public interest. It would acknowledge that regulators would be ever hopeful that interest groups, government(s), review courts, and the general public would regard their decisions as being consistent with the attainment of the public interest. However, it is more concerned with noting the independence of regulators and analysing their interactions with the regulated. Both models explicitly examine the role of the state. Whereas capture theory regards the state as a passive victim of interest groups, bargaining theory views regulators as independent, with desires and interests that cannot be ignored in developing an understanding of the processes of social change.

CONCLUSION

This chapter has examined five different theoretical approaches to the study of industrial relations. Dunlop's systems model provides a shell within which industrial relations phenomena can be analysed. The model is poorly developed with respect to processes, the motivation of actors, and the role of the state and it downplays the importance of conflict. Kochan, McKersie, and Cappelli's modifications, though interesting with respect to the level of analysis, do not overcome these problems.

Fox's straw-man model of industrial relations pluralism is also poorly developed. His firm-based model encounters problems when it is generalized to society as a whole, and is even more inadequate than Dunlop's model with respect to the role of the state. Furthermore, Fox and Flanders find it difficult to distinguish change from anomie. It was suggested that the North American political science model of the 1950s could be adapted to the study of industrial relations.

There are a number of difficulties associated with Marxist approaches to the study of industrial relations. The first and major difficulty concerns the amorphous breadth of Marxism and the associated view that industrial relations is too narrow an area for Marxist scholarship. It also encounters difficulties with respect to the level of analysis: should it be firm based or societal based? What is the nature of conflict within capitalism? and should unions pursue short-term economic goals rather than revolutionary change? Marxism explicitly tackles the role of the state, a dependent variable acting as an agent of capital to enhance capitalist reproduction and/or incorporate and tame trade unions.

Corporatism, unlike Marxism, views the state as an independent variable seeking to replace conflict and competition with consensus and co-operation in furtherance of the common good. The state incorporates representatives of capital and labour who in turn discipline their constituent parts to ensure the attainment of the common good. The major criticisms of corporatism are the (contradictory) possibility that force may be necessary to ensure 'consensus', the aggregated societal-based level of analysis, and the assumption that representative bodies have the power and authority to control affiliates.

Theories of regulation are concerned with examining the relationship between economic agents and the various state entities that regulate their activities. Regulation theories employ a disaggregated societal-based level of analysis. Capture theory postulates that the regulatory agency will be captured by the regulated and will serve their interests rather than those of society as a whole. Bargaining theory, on the other hand, views the regulatory agency as an independent variable that, in seeking to lead the regulated down an ideal path of regulation, enters into bargains with them.

NOTES

1 For literature in this area see Ehrlick and Wooton (1980), Nicholls (1974), McFarland (1969), Connolly (1969), Barkin (1971), Kelso (1978), and Hyman (1978).
2 Some limited attempts were made by American writers. See Kerr (1964) and Kerr *et al.* (1973, pp. 270–7).
3 In the literature it is referred to as 'the theory of job regulation' or 'the Oxford approach'.
4 Flanders (1965) and Clegg (1975) are also important writers in this tradition. For reviews of developments within British industrial relations pluralism see Hyman (1978, pp. 22–36) and Wood and Elliot (1979). Hyman and Fryer (1975) describe pluralism as 'a process of antagonistic co-operation'.
5 Fox has mounted attacks on industrial relations pluralism on two flanks; the literature refers to this as the 'radical perspective'. For a review see Crouch (1982, pp. 24–8), Hyman (1978), Hyman and Fryer (1975, pp. 167–70), Hyman and Brough (1975, pp. 157–83), and Goldthorpe (1977).
6 This of course is the message of theories of dual and segmented labour markets.

7 See Hyman and Brough (1975, pp. 173−8), Goldthorpe (1969, 1977), and Eldridge (1971, pp. 73−119).

8 In addition to textual references see Hyman (1971, 1975, 1980). Also see Allen (1971). For some Australian writing in this tradition see Bray and Taylor (1986).

9 In a geographically large nation regional differences may also be important (city versus country, large states versus small states). It may also be appropriate to examine conflict between indigenous members of the population and immigrants, religious and ethnic groups, and male domination in a patriarchal society.

10 Hyman (1971) tackles the issue of whether unions are capable of achieving revolutionary change. Also see Crouch (1982, pp. 127−38).

11 For a debate concerning the role of the labour movement see Lenin (1970) and Perlman (1949).

12 See for example Miliband (1973), Jessop (1977), and Stepan (1978, pp. 17−26).

13 Marxists interpret these systems to be synonymous with the needs of capital. See Panitch (1977, 1980, 1981). For a critique of Panitch see Booth (1982).

14 Crouch's definition concentrates on the bargaining between the state and unions, and ignores capital/employers. He is apparently uninterested in examining the concessions gained by capital from the state outside the labour market. See Crouch (1979a, pp. 188−96) and Crouch (1977, pp. 262−9).

15 For further discussion of the similarities between corporatism and pluralism see Martin (1983).

16 Panitch (1977, pp. 81−3) maintains that British attempts at incomes policies floundered because of the response of the shopfloor.

17 For further discussion of capture theory see Bernstein (1955), Posner (1974), and Goldberg (1976).

18 See Wilson (1971, 1974, 1978, 1980), Joskow (1974), Baldwin (1975), and Porter and Sagansky (1976).

CHAPTER 2

The Early 1980s

In Chapter 1 corporatism was depicted as an aggregated societal-based model where representatives of the state, capital, and unions sought to replace competition and conflict with co-operation and consensus in pursuit of the so-called common good. Two theoretical and conceptual problems need to be examined when attempting to apply theories of corporatism to Australia.

The first relates to the peculiarities of the state in Australia, in particular to the constitutional protection afforded to the Australian Conciliation and Arbitration Commission. As students of Australian industrial relations are well aware, the Commonwealth government, with some important exceptions such as its own employees and territories, does not have a direct industrial relations power. The Commonwealth government's major industrial relations power is section 51, paragraph xxxv, of the Australian Constitution:

The Parliament shall, subject to this Constitution, have the power to make laws for the peace, order and good government of the Commonwealth with respect to ... Conciliation and Arbitration for the prevention and settlement of industrial disputes extending beyond the limits of any one State.

In other words, section 51, paragraph xxxv, forces the Commonwealth government to delegate industrial relations powers to industrial tribunals, the most significant of which is the commission, which have available to them powers of conciliation and arbitration to settle and prevent interstate industrial disputes. The constitutional protection afforded the commission vis-à-vis the Commonwealth government means that it is inappropriate to regard the state in monolithic terms, as is implied by corporatism.[1]

At the Commonwealth level, then, we can distinguish at least two different arms of the state — the Commonwealth government and the commission. It is therefore possible to identify two different models, or versions, of corporatism which could occur in Australia. The first is where the commission adopts a corporatist model in defiance of or against the wishes of the Commonwealth government. Such a situation occurred during the Fraser ministries of late 1975 to early 1981. The commission administered a centralized system of industrial relations regulation that was based on wage indexation, despite the opposition of the Fraser government. The second model is where the commission and the Commonwealth government both agree on the need for a corporatist policy — and presumably the broad contours of its implementation. Two such occasions occurred when the commission and the Fraser government agreed on the need for a wages freeze at the end of 1982 and when the commission endorsed the various versions of the Accord, which have been a feature of the Hawke ministries (see Chapter 3). (It is difficult to see how a corporatist policy could be pursued by a Commonwealth government were the commission opposed to such a policy, given the commission's constitutional powers with respect to industrial relations regulation. Equally though, would it be possible for a Commonwealth government, or more particularly a political party, to gain political advantage by advocating a corporatist policy if it believed that the commission desired implementation of such a policy?)

The second problem associated with applying corporatism to Australia concerns the involvement or role of capital/employers. Corporatism is predicated on peak-level negotiations and decisions being made by the state, unions, and capital/ employers. However, during both the wage indexation experiment of the commission from 1975 to 1981, and the Accord(s) from 1983 to 1986 (see Chapters 3 and 5), national-level employers have played a relatively minor role and have had a limited input into the decisions that have been made. In both periods, when wage rises were generally linked to movements in prices, national-level employers argued for zero or minimal increases in wages or for wages to be linked to movements in long-run national productivity.

Given the fragmented, or non-monolithic, nature of the state, and the limited role of national-level employers in the decision-making process, it may be appropriate to agree with those commentators who have depicted antipodean experiments with corporatism as being partially or quasi-corporatist (Loveday, 1984; Singleton, 1985; Stewart, 1985; Colebatch, 1986; Gerritsen, 1986; McEachern, 1986; Pemberton and Davis, 1986; Stilwell, 1986).

This chapter firstly examines the 'quasi-corporatist' wage indexation experiment developed by the Australian Conciliation and Arbitration Commission. This is followed by an account of the abandonment of wage indexation in the middle of 1981 and the concomitant development of a (societal) pluralistic, decentralized system of industrial relations regulation. The chapter then examines the wages freeze and the return to centralization which occurred in December 1982.

WAGE INDEXATION

At the beginning of the 1980s the system of industrial relations regulation in Australia was centralized and known as *wage indexation*. That wages would be linked to movements in prices was the prima facie expectation. The commission had introduced wage indexation on 30 April 1975 in an attempt to arrest the economic problems of increasing levels of inflation and unemployment experienced by Australia from the mid-1970s. The commission was prepared to consider adjusting wages for movements in the consumer price index (CPI) each quarter (after September 1978, adjustments were six-monthly) as a means of overcoming Australia's economic, industrial, and social problems if, and only if, wage rises from other sources were kept to a minimum. In its original wage indexation decision of 30 April 1975 the commission warned that 'violation even by a small section of industry whether in the award or non-award area would put at risk the future of indexation for all' (NWC, 30 April 1975, p. 37).

The commission enunciated a set of guidelines to accompany wage indexation. Besides regular quarterly (after September 1978, six-monthly) hearings to consider the extent to which wages should be adjusted for changes in prices, the commission envisaged the hearing of an annual case to consider and/or take account of movements in national productivity (it is interesting to note that no such case was mounted by the Australian Council of Trade Unions (ACTU) during the six-year life of wage indexation). The commission's guidelines provided scope for exceptional wage rises to occur outside national wage cases — for example, changes in work value, catch-up of community movements (for those who had missed out on the wage-round prior to indexation's introduction), anomalies (added in May 1976), and inequities (added in September 1978).

Wage indexation lasted six years, from April 1975 to July 1981. Table 2.1 summarizes the various 'indexation' decisions of the commission in this period. The commission awarded full indexation in seven of its nineteen decisions (the 6.4 per cent awarded after the publication of the December 1975 CPI provided full indexation for both the September and December 1975 quarters). On other occasions the commission awarded either partial or plateau increases.

Besides these 'indexation' increases, an important work-value round began in the middle of 1978. Waterside workers gained a work-value increase in the vicinity of $8 per week, with similar increases flowing to workers in other industries and sectors of the economy. In its decision in the January 1980 national wage case the commission estimated that approximately 18 per cent of the workforce had received such increases, in its July 1980 decision the commission increased this figure to 34.1 per cent, and in its April 1981 decision the commission found that 80 per cent of the workforce had gained the increases. Two things should be noted about this work-value round: firstly its speed — three years to flow to 80 per cent of the workforce; secondly most of the flow occurred late in the round, between July 1980 and April 1981.

Table 2.2 provides information on wage indexation increases as a percentage of the change in total wages in the period

Table 2.1   Alterations to Total Wage under Wage Indexation, 1975—81

Date	CPI Change (%)	Wage Change
1975 March	3.6	3.6%
June	3.5	3.5%
September	0.8	Nil
December	5.6	(5.6% + 0.8% =) 6.4%
1976 March	3.0	3.0% to $125 per week; $3.80 thereafter
June	2.5	2.5% to $98 per week; then $2.50 to $98—$166 per week; 1.5% thereafter
September	2.2	2.2%
December	6.0	$5.70
1977 March	2.3	1.9% to $200 per week; $3.80 thereafter
June	2.4	2.0%
September	2.0	1.5%
December	2.3	1.5% to $170 per week; $2.60 thereafter
1978 March	1.3	1.3%
June/September	4.0	4.0%
December/March 79	4.0	3.2%
1979 June/September	5.0	4.5%
December/March 80	5.3	4.2%
1980 June/September	4.7	3.7%
December/March 81	4.5	3.6%

Source: National wage case decisions.

1975—81. The table shows that the commission was largely successful in ensuring that 'indexation' increases were the major source of wage movements in Australia in these years. In the early years of wage indexation, in excess of 90 per cent of wage movements for both males and females resulted from the

Table 2.2 Wage Indexation Increases as a Percentage of Change in Total Wage, 1975–81

Year Ended		Male (%)	Female (%)
August	1976	92	94
August	1977	94	96
June	1978	98	99
December	1978	89	97
June	1979	86	95
January	1980	86	96
July	1980	81	86
January	1981	83	70
May	1981	91	79

Source: Australian Bureau of Statistics, *Wage Rate Indexes* (*Preliminary*), Catalogue No. 6311.0.

'indexation' national wage case decisions of the commission. In the second half of the period the figure declines to slightly more than 80 per cent for males and slightly less than 80 per cent for females, which mainly reflects the flow of the $8 work-value round.

Table 2.3 provides details of the respective submissions of the Commonwealth government and the major private employers during the life of wage indexation. No information has been provided for the December 1980–March 1981 quarters because the commission had previously decided to (automatically) award 80 per cent indexation (NWC, 7 April 1981).

The Whitlam Labor government was in power for the hearing of the first three cases and, with the exception of its ambivalence concerning the September 1975 quarter, supported full wage indexation. The Fraser coalition government was in office from November 1975. The table shows that, with a few exceptions, both the Fraser government and the private employers opposed the granting of wage indexation, advocating nil or minimal increases. Table 2.3 verifies that wage indexation was a quasi-corporatist policy operated by the commission in opposition to the stated position of both the Fraser government and the private employers.

Table 2.3   Commonwealth Government and Private Employers' Submissions during Wage Indexation, March 1975 to June–September 1980

Date	CPI Change (%)	Commonwealth Government Submission	Private Employers' Submission
1975 March	3.6	3.6%	Nil
June	3.5	3.5%	Nil
September	0.8	Nil or 0.8%	Nil
December[a]	5.6 (+0.8)	3.2%	4.0%
1976 March	3.0	Flat $2.80	Nil or minimal
June	2.5	Nil or 0.75%	Moderate or minimal
September	2.2	About 0.6%	Moderate or minimal
December	6.0	Flat $2.90	Minimal or $2.50
1977 March	2.3	Nil	Nil
June	2.4	Nil	Nil
September	2.0	Nil	Nil
1978 March	1.3	Nil	Nil
June/ September	4.0	Nil or small %	Nil
December/ March 79	4.0	Nil	Nil
1979 June/ September	5.0	3.0%	Nil
December/ March 80	5.3	Nil	Nil
1980 June/ September[b]	4.7	Nil	Nil

Sources: National wage case decisions and Plowman (1981, p. 137).
[a] Whitlam Labor government replaced by Fraser Liberal–National Party coalition government.
[b] Submissions for December 1980–March 1981 are excluded because of the commission's introduction of 80 per cent automatic indexation.

DECENTRALIZATION REPLACES INDEXATION

In the national wage case decision of January 1981 the commission made the following statement, which summarized its views on the wage indexation experiment it had introduced in April 1975:

What was envisaged in April 1975 tentatively and cautiously as a voluntary and co-operative venture to deal with a difficult industrial and economic situation in an orderly way seems to have worked more or less satisfactorily for some four years. But in the last eighteen months the system has made heavy weather industrially, and we do not believe that it is any longer viable in its present form (NWC, 9 January 1981, p. 12).

The commission identified what it regarded to be the major reasons for the breakdown of wage indexation: the granting of less than full CPI adjustments (though, as Table 2.1 shows, this practice had started in 1976, early in the period of indexation's 'satisfactory operation'), the persistent non-compliance of some of the parties, and the lack of support of both the Fraser government and the private employers. From the second half of 1979 the commission had consistently expressed concern about the lack of support for wage indexation, and indicated on more than one occasion that it was on the brink of abandoning the system. The commission's president, Sir John Moore, initiated a series of conferences with the parties throughout the period mid-1979 to mid-1981, and the commission developed two new sets of guidelines in what turned out to be vain attempts to save wage indexation.

The commission's wage indexation system was based on the assumption that national wage cases were to be the major source of changes in wages and/or movements in working conditions; wage increases from other sources were required to be kept to a minimum. During 1980 and 1981, however, this assumption was increasingly under attack from three sources. First, there was the work-value round that has already been referred to; in the period July 1980 to April 1981, 46 per cent of the workforce gained work-value increases. Second, unions in the metal trades initiated a campaign for the introduction of a 35-hour week in 1980. In what eventually turned out to be a forlorn attempt to gain control over the shorter hours campaign the commission indicated in its April 1981 national wage case decision that it was prepared to consider applications for reducing standard hours of work under the national productivity principles inherent in the guidelines (NWC, 7 April 1981, p. 47). Third, in the early 1980s Australia experienced what turned out to be a short-lived mining and resources boom. Increasing numbers of employers in growth areas of the economy were prepared to offer and/or pay higher wages than those sanctioned by the commission's wage indexation guidelines.

In May, June, and July 1981 a number of unions and employers, in both the private and the public sectors, negotiated wage increases in the vicinity of $20 per week. In some cases these increases were accompanied by the use of industrial action. Given the frustrations and problems that the commission had experienced over the previous two years (its threats to abandon indexation, the use of conferences, and the introduction of revised principles), and a realization that a new wage-round had begun — a wage-round which it had played no part in determining — it is not surprising that on 31 July 1981 the commission formally brought wage indexation to an end. It also announced that it would not countenance hearing another national wage case before February 1982 (NWC, 31 July 1981, p. 3).

The economic growth associated with the mining and resources boom, combined with the actions of some of the parties, resulted in the replacement of wage indexation with a more flexible and decentralized system of industrial relations regulation, a system in which the commission's role was substantially less influential and prominent than it had hitherto been. After 31 July 1981 the parties increasingly entered into direct negotiations with each other. Negotiations were conducted on an award-by-award basis, with many agreements being ratified by the appropriate tribunals in the form of consent awards.

We will examine two key cases of the period. The first concerns an attempt by employers and unions in the transport industry to have the commission ratify an agreement to increase wages by $20 per week based on so-called changes in work value. The commission refused ratification because it doubted the veracity of the claims concerning the work-value changes, a lengthy dispute had preceded the agreement, and there was apprehension that the $20 would flow on to other transport workers. In reaching this decision the commission also noted 'that there is an obvious overlap between changes in work value and national productivity movements' (the former occurring at the micro level; the latter, at the macro level) and indicated that it would be prepared to convene a national wage case ahead of the February 1982 date it had set itself in abandoning wage indexation on 31 July 1981 (Transport Workers Award, 1 September 1981, p. 17). This preparedness to convene an 'early' national wage case might be seen as being influenced by the commission's ambivalence over the earlier decision to abandon wage indexation. Perhaps too the commission feared that if work-value cum productivity changes began to flow through the system, its ability to distribute national productivity changes via national wage cases — which the commission has believed it should do since the prices plus productivity formula of the 1961 *Basic Wage* case (97 CAR 376) — would be reduced. None of the parties took up the commission's offer to convene an 'early' national wage case, however.

The second case, which undoubtedly attracted the most interest and attention in the period, was the agreement negotiated in the metal trades and ratified by the commission on 18 December 1981. The agreement contained five key elements:

1 An increase in the supplementary payment (an exercise in absorbing over-award pay into the award) to the fitter of $9.30 per week (with proportionate increases for other classifications)
2 A $25 per week increase for the fitter
3 A mid-term adjustment of $14 per week for the fitter from 1 June 1982, unless 'there is an unforeseen change of an extraordinary nature to the economic circumstances'
4 The introduction of a 38-hour week from 15 March 1982
5 A no-extra-claims clause during the (twelve-month) life of the agreement.

The commission's preparedness to ratify this agreement — whereas it had earlier refused ratification in the transport industry — in a sense represented its acknowledgement, from December 1981, that it would be pointless to stand against the forces of decentralization that dominated Australian industrial relations.

Early in 1982 the ACTU initiated a national wage case wherein an award — for what the ACTU called the 'community standard', established since the end of indexation — was sought for those workers who had not yet received an increase. The reintroduction of automatic, quarterly cost of living adjustments, beginning with the December 1981 quarter, was also sought. In handing down its decision the commission pointed out that the ACTU had not taken up its offer, in its decision concerning transport workers on 1 September 1981, to consider the hearing of 'a general wage adjustment' in a national wage case. Unions, many of whose actions were co-ordinated by the ACTU, had pursued a decentralized negotiating campaign (NWC, 14 May 1982, p. 3). With respect to the ACTU's claim concerning the establishment of a 'community standard' the commission noted that while nearly 75 per cent of employees, or over 80 per cent of award workers, had obtained wage increases since the end of indexation, no 'community standard' as such had been established. The commission pointed to the variability and diversity of the increases that had been obtained (NWC, 14 May 1982, pp. 16, 17). The commission seems to have expected that it would only be a matter of time before wage increases would flow to those employees who had not obtained a post-indexation increase.

The commission also turned down the ACTU's claim concerning the reintroduction of wage indexation, giving three reasons for its decision. First, as far as the commission was concerned, a system of wage indexation implied that national wage cases should be the prime and only source of wage increases, increases which were to be based on changes in prices and national productivity. As most of the wage increases negotiated in the period after 31 July 1981 had been based on anticipated price and/or productivity increases, a return to wage indexation would involve double-counting and impose a cost burden which, the commission believed, the Australian economy could ill afford to bear. Second, notwithstanding the ACTU's call for the re-establishment of a system of wage indexation, the commission was far from convinced that the parties desired to return to wage indexation and/or had the appropriate degree of 'collective responsibility' to make it work (NWC, 14 May 1982, p. 51). It should again be remembered that the commission had spent two frustrating years, from mid-1979 to mid-1981, in an unsuccessful attempt to gain the support of the parties for its system of wage indexation. Given this experience the commission may have had good reason to doubt that the parties would adhere to the strictures implied by a regime of wage indexation. Third, the commission said it wanted more time to determine an appropriate course of action for the future. Again, it appears that the commission wanted to wait for the metal trades agreement to run its course (in May 1982 the agreement still had six months to go) before embarking on any 'new' system of industrial relations regulation. The decision stated that Sir John Moore would convene a conference on 17 August 1982 'to review the future of wage fixing procedures raised in this case' (NWC, 14 May 1982, p. 57). A series of meetings were held in August and September, but achieved little; private employers and the Fraser coalition government opposed the ACTU's desire to return to a centralized system of industrial relations regulation based on wage indexation (Mulvey, 1983, pp. 70–1).

WAGES FREEZE AND A RETURN TO CENTRALIZATION

In the second half of 1982, drought and a world recession combined to severely strain the Australian economy. By the end of 1982 the inflation rate exceeded 10 per cent and the unemployment rate was approaching that figure. The condition of the economy was such that there were strong rumours that many workers and their employers had agreed to work short hours (a four-day week), with less-than-award provisions, in an effort to stave off retrenchments (Mulvey, 1983, p. 71).

On 4 December 1982 a by-election was held in the seat of Flinders following the retirement of the deputy leader of the federal Liberal Party, Phillip Lynch. While a close result was anticipated, political pundits predicted a Labor victory, owing to the condition of the economy and the Fraser ministry's internal divisions and wranglings. The government of the day decided to campaign around the need for a 'wages pause', or 'wages freeze', and in the process turned away from its previous commitment to a decentralized, case-by-case approach to industrial relations regulation and wage determination. By directing attention to the need for a freeze the Fraser government could displace criticism and rationalize the downturn of the economy in terms of the activities of unions and their campaigns for increased wages.

The Fraser government won the Flinders by-election.[2] Subsequently, at the Premiers Conference held on 7 December 1982, the Commonwealth, state, and territory governments all agreed on the need to implement a wages freeze, and announced their intention to introduce appropriate legislation in their respective jurisdictions.[3] Because of the constraints of the Australian Constitution the Commonwealth government lacked power to introduce such legislation with respect to federal awards in the private sector. At the end of December 1982 the federal government (in combination with the state and territory governments) urged the commission to implement a twelve months' wage freeze (some state governments preferred a six months' freeze). While the ACTU did not oppose the need for corrective action, it suggested that the commission delay its decision until there had been a national economic conference involving Commonwealth and state governments, employers, and the ACTU, 'aimed at determining a course of action to attack the current economic position' (NWC, 23 December 1982, p. 32) — a proposal rejected by the Fraser government.

In reaching its decision the commission expressed concern about the deteriorating condition of the economy and noted that all governments were united on the need for a wages freeze. It quoted, with seeming favour, from a submission by Victoria 'that the pause is the beginnings of a process of re-establishing a centralised wage fixing system' (NWC, 23 December 1982, p. 10). The commission decided to introduce a wages freeze for six months rather than the twelve months recommended by the Commonwealth government,[4] because 'In the current changing economic climate it is more difficult than usual to make economic judgment bearing on a substantial period ahead' (NWC, 23 December 1982, p. 12). The commission would convene a national wage case in late June 1983 to consider what action should be taken in future.

The wages freeze is an example of the second type of quasi-corporatism referred to in the introduction to this chapter. Putting to one side the difference between the Fraser government and the commission concerning the length of the freeze, it constitutes a situation where the Commonwealth government and the commission agreed on the need for a quasi-corporatist policy with which to respond to Australia's economic and industrial relations problems. It is also interesting to note that the private employers did not find it difficult to support a quasi-corporatist policy that posited the need for a wages freeze.

CONCLUSION

Two points can be made in conclusion. The first concerns the flexibility or adaptability of Australian industrial relations. At the beginning of the 1980s Australia was subject to a quasi-corporatist policy based on wage indexation. Under wage indexation the Conciliation and Arbitration Commission hoped that national wage cases would be the major source of movements in wages and working conditions. As Table 2.2 demonstrates, the commission by and large succeeded in achieving this objective. On 31 July 1981 the commission abandoned wage indexation and Australia adopted a (societal) pluralistic (see Chapter 1) decentralized system of industrial relations regulation. Changes to wages and other working conditions (such as reductions in the length of the standard working week) resulted primarily from direct negotiations of the parties on a case-by-case basis, with the commission and other tribunals playing a relatively minor role. In December 1982 Australia returned to a centralized quasi-corporatist system based on a zero-wage norm.

What should be noted here is the ability of the Australian industrial relations system to switch from a quasi-corporatist system based in the main on wage indexation, to a (societal) pluralistic, flexible, decentralized system, and then to an alternative quasi-corporatist system enshrining a wages freeze. Australian industrial relations, in this period at least, demonstrated a certain flexibility.

The second point concerns the commission's attitude, or commitment, to wage indexation as a tool of industrial relations regulation. Since mid-1979 the commission had experienced problems in convincing parties of the economic and industrial relations advantages which flowed from observing the strictures inherent in a system of wage indexation. Despite these problems it will be argued here that the commission still believed that it was only through observing the dictates associated with a system of wage indexation that Australia could ever hope to solve its economic and industrial relations problems. The commission, of course, had expressed such views in its various national wage case decisions during the wage indexation regime in the period 1975−81. In its September 1981 decision in the transport industry the commission had broadly hinted at this, or that at a minimum national wage cases should be restored to their former prominence as a source of wage movements. In the May 1982 national wage case the commission, in noting the problems with extracting an appropriate level of commitment from the parties, said:

The Commission has from time to time during the period of indexation emphasised the benefits, both industrial and economic, to be gained from a centralised and orderly system of wage fixation which gave high priority to the maintenance of real wages of all wage and salary earners, the weak and the strong (NWC, 14 May 1982, p. 47).

Virtually the same personnel who constituted the leadership of the commission in the period 1975−81 were still in office at the end of 1982. If they had believed in the efficacy of wage indexation for the period 1975−81, why would they not believe in its efficacy at the end of 1982? Would not the events of the second half of 1981 and 1982 — decentralized wage determination followed by a deteriorating economy — have convinced them of the wisdom of having pursued wage indexation from 1975 to 1981, and of the need to reinstate such a system in the near future? In the following chapter, which examines developments in 1983, it will be argued that the commission wished to re-introduce wage indexation.

NOTES

1 It should also be noted that we are ignoring any theoretical problems posed for corporatism by the existence of state and territory governments alongside the Commonwealth government, as well as the existence of superior courts.

2 For further details see Kelly (1984, Chapter 17).
3 For details concerning these legislative initiatives see NWC, 23 December 1982, Appendix, pp. 22–33.
4 The freeze lasted nine months.

CHAPTER 3

The Golden Age of Consensus

Chapter 2 described how the Australian Conciliation and Arbitration Commission introduced a wages freeze at the end of December 1982 in response to the various problems of the economy. In 1983 the economy further deteriorated, with both the unemployment and inflation rates exceeding 10 per cent. Many believed Australia was experiencing its worst economic crisis since the Depression of the 1930s.

Coalition Prime Minister Malcolm Fraser decided to call an early election (for 5 March 1983) on, as it happened, the same day (3 February) that Bob Hawke replaced Bill Hayden as leader of the Australian Labor Party (ALP). Fraser seems to have based his decision on an expectation that the economy would deteriorate further in 1983, the favourable result in the Flinders by-election, and a hope of gaining political advantage from anticipated ructions within the ALP associated with Hawke and Hayden's struggle for the ALP leadership.

Bob Hawke began his career as an advocate for the Australian Council of Trade Unions (ACTU) in the latter part of the 1950s. He was an aggressive and imaginative advocate who quickly developed a reputation as a 'fixer', a person who could help resolve and/or bring about an end to seemingly intractable industrial disputes. Besides establishing contacts and friendships within unions and the ALP, Hawke also developed friendships with many of Australia's leading businessmen and captains of industry. Hawke projected himself as a man of consensus. In 1980 he resigned his position as ACTU president to successfully contest a federal parliamentary seat on behalf of the ALP.

On assuming ALP leadership in February 1983 Hawke based his electoral strategy on replacing the so-called confrontationist and divisive policies of the Fraser government with a (corporatist) programme of national reconstruction based on consensus and co-operation. The Hawke-led ALP quickly negotiated the Accord with the ACTU — something Hayden had unsuccessfully sought — as a first step in the direction of consensus, or corporatist, politics. Hawke pledged that if he won the forthcoming election he would hold a national economic summit conference of governments, employers, unions, and various interest groups which, via consensus and co-operation, would seek to devise a programme to achieve economic recovery.

The Accord, the proposed summit, and the general philosophical commitment to consensus have been viewed as important factors in explaining the 1983 electoral success of the Hawke-led ALP.[1] After the election, and the April summit, the Australian Conciliation and Arbitration Commission reintroduced a centralized system of wage determination based on wage indexation. Hawke's vision for Australia resulted in the reintroduction of a method of industrial relations regulation which had been abandoned only two years earlier.

This chapter examines and comments on the Accord, the April 1983 National Economic Summit Conference, and events following the summit, and finally offers a critique of wage indexation.

THE ACCORD (MARK I)

The Accord is a bipartite agreement between the ALP and the ACTU which was negotiated during an election campaign in the context of a stagflationary economy where both inflation and unemployment rates were in excess of 10 per cent. The Accord specifies a series of policy measures, for implementation in the event of success at the 1983 polls. The Accord's key concept is that only by pursuing consensus-based policies can Australia ever hope to achieve economic recovery. The Accord spends much time in singing the praises of prices and incomes policies as the most effective way to bring about economic growth; for example

a mutually agreed policy on prices and incomes in Australia for implementation by a Labor government ... offers by far the best prospect of enabling Australia to experience prolonged higher rates of economic and employment growth, and accompanying growth in living standards, without incurring the circumscribing penalty of higher inflation, by providing for resolution of conflicting income claims at lower levels of inflation than would otherwise be the case. With inflation control being achieved in this way, budgetary and monetary policies may be responsibly set to promote economic and employment growth, thus enabling unemployment to be reduced and living standards to rise (Accord, p. 2).

Not surprisingly the Accord rejected the Fraser government's wages freeze,[2] claiming that it was one-sided and that a reduction in wages would reduce demand and 'accentuate economic recession and increase unemployment' (Accord, p. 2). The Accord talks about the need for a comprehensive prices and incomes policy and of how it is inappropriate and inequitable to confine incomes policies to wage and salary earners. Under the Accord, not only would wage and salary earners have their incomes controlled but there would also be controls on prices and non-wage incomes.

With respect to wages and salaries the Accord advocates a return to a centralized system based on wage indexation — to a system which the commission had abandoned not two years earlier, in July 1981. It is interesting to note, moreover, that the Accord, in praising the efficacy of prices and incomes policies, does not mention Australia's experience with wage indexation in the period 1975–81. In championing centralization the Accord says that 'the maintenance of real wages is agreed to be a key objective ... over time', that wage and salary earners should share in increased national productivity, and 'that there should be no extra claims except where special and extraordinary circumstances exist' (Accord, p. 5).

As well as the need for a prices and incomes policy the Accord specifies a number of supporting policies which would be pursued by an ALP government. If elected, the ALP would introduce taxation and fiscal reforms to 'ease the tax burden on low and middle income earners', 'adopt tough new measures to smash the tax avoidance industry', reform company tax laws 'to ensure that companies pay their fair share of tax on income earned in Australia and overseas', 'reduce the relative incidence of indirect taxation because of its regressive and inflationary nature', and take appropriate action to eliminate poverty and increase the social wage of low-income earners. Other reforms to be introduced by an ALP government were in the areas of industrial relations legislation, industrial development, and technological change — in particular, interventionist or industry policies designed 'to develop a viable manufacturing sector', immigration, social security, occupational health and safety, education, health, and 'the restoration of good industrial relations' with Commonwealth government employees. The Accord also envisaged the creation of consultative bodies constituting representatives from the national employers, as well as the government and the ACTU, to co-operatively plan for the future. The Accord is silent on the various employment and related problems experienced by Australian women.

The Accord was designed to satisfy the short-term needs of both the ALP and the ACTU. The most important need of the ALP, of course, was to win the forthcoming election. By entering into an agreement with the ACTU, which linked economic growth and recovery to consensus, the ALP hoped to convince the electorate of its capacity to govern Australia through the difficult economic times ahead. If nothing else, the Accord provided a plan of action for the future. The Accord, by linking economic recovery and consensus, made it difficult for opponents to mount criticisms of the ALP's electoral strategy. Critics of the Accord could expect the retort that they were opposed to economic growth and recovery, that they were divisive, and antipathetic to the long-term survival needs of Australia.

The ACTU derived two major advantages from the Accord. First, with the ALP in power the ACTU could expect more favourable treatment, as well as its desired legislative changes, than it had experienced when Fraser was in power. Second, the Accord heralded significant industrial relations advantages, the most significant of which was the prospect of replacing a wages freeze with wage indexation. In the context of the worst economic crisis since the Depression of the 1930s, with unemployment rates in excess of 10 per cent, the reintroduction of wage indexation would constitute a significant victory for the ACTU. Moreover, whereas in the Fraser years wage indexation had been criticized and viewed as a major source of Australia's economic problems, the Accord — and if elected, a Hawke ALP government — regarded wage indexation as a key element in economic salvation.

The previous chapter advanced the proposition that the commission wished to re-establish a centralized system of wage determination based on wage indexation. Given the constitutional protection afforded the commission, wage indexation could never be implemented if the commission was opposed to its reintroduction. If the commission decided to implement a wages norm less than that implied by wage indexation, or a decentralized system of industrial relations regulation, the Accord would quickly disintegrate. The argument advanced here is that both a Hawke-led ALP and the ACTU, with their not inconsiderable knowledge of industrial relations and an ability to read the desires of the commission from its previous decisions, assumed that the commission wanted to reintroduce wage indexation. If this analysis is correct, the major skill of the Accord was the ability of the ALP (and the ACTU) to gain political kudos from appearing to be responsible for a policy which the commission itself wished to put in place.[3]

The Accord rests on the assumption that corporatist, or consensus-based, societies that have adopted incomes policies have achieved better economic performance than those societies that have not adopted or pursued such policies. The Accord states that

It is extremely significant that the [OECD] countries which have managed to fare better in this time of economic adversity, particularly by keeping unemployment to relatively low levels, have been notably those countries which have eschewed monetarism and have instead placed substantial importance on developing prices and incomes policies by consultation (Accord, p. 2).

In the discussion which follows, corporatist, or consensus-based, policies are equated with the use of incomes policies. This assumption is made because the Accord itself links economic success to incomes policies based on co-operation and, as Chapter 1 noted, the emergence of corporatism as an area of theoretical discourse was associated with the use of incomes policies in the 1960s and 1970s.

The usual method used by those who claim that corporatist incomes policies are more successful economic-management tools than policies such as monetarism (and Keynesianism?)[4] is to rank Organization for Economic Co-operation and Development (OECD) countries by economic performance — using 'objective' measures such as growth, inflation, and unemployment rates — and then to ascertain the extent to which the respective countries could be regarded as being corporatist. This ascertaining is exceptionally subjective.

Alternative qualitative measures have been attempted. Bruno and Sachs, for example, have devised a four-part index in an attempt to measure levels of corporatism within and across nations. They are

the extent to which wage negotiations proceed on the national level rather than the plant level; the power of national level organisations vis-à-vis their constituent members; the degree of organisation on the employer side; and the power of plant-level union stewards (the more powerful they are, the less corporatism there is) (Bruno and Sachs, 1985, pp. 222–3).

Notwithstanding the development of such 'objective' measures researchers are still required to make subjective assessments of a particular country. This is the case especially when knowledge of and/or a feeling for the nuances and subtleties of industrial relations in various overseas countries are/is limited.

For example Bruno and Sachs have allocated a very low corporatism score — actually zero — to Australia (Bruno and Sachs, 1985, pp. 226–8). However, it could be argued that Australia should receive a very high score against their corporatist index. First, given the existence of national wage cases under the control of the commission — and the use of wage indexation from April 1975 to July 1981 should be remembered in this context — wages in Australia are determined at 'the national level rather than the plant level'. Second, affiliates have given the ACTU the authority to help defend and advance their collective rights and interests (Dabscheck, 1977). Third, the formation of the Confederation of Australian Industry (CAI) in 1977 as the single, peak federal-level employer group in Australia would seem to indicate that there is 'organisation on the employer side', though, as has already been argued in Chapters 1 and 2, employers/business/capital in Australia are more fragmented than the formation of the CAI would suggest (and presumably this could be a problem in other 'corporatist' nations). Fourth, Australia does not have any well-developed system of 'plant-level union stewards'. Depending, then, on how one interprets the 'degree of organisation on the employer side' Australia might receive a score of either three or four out of four against the Bruno and Sachs corporatist index.

Misgivings have also been expressed about problems associated with cross-country comparisons. Gruen has argued that

There are too many uncontrolled — and uncontrollable — variables in [a cross-country] comparison over two fixed time periods to carry conviction that the investigator has succeeded in isolating the effect of incomes policy and of consensus on the growth—unemployment—inflation performance of these different economies (Gruen, 1983, p. 2).

Bruno and Sachs have pointed to limitations associated with unemployment measures in several OECD countries:

In Austria, Finland, Germany, and Switzerland, outmigration of foreign workers hid some of the decline in employment after 1973. In Japan, women workers withdrew from the labor force upon job loss and thus were not counted among the unemployed. And in Sweden, extensive official worker retraining programs kept unemployed workers out of the official statistics (Bruno and Sachs, 1985, p. 219).

In addition, the economic success of incomes-policy countries seems to diminish when a longer time horizon is adopted. Hughes, for example, has pointed out that

The striking thing about post-war advocacy of incomes policy is the way in which the star countries have changed over the years. For a long time the Netherlands was held up as an example, partly because of an agreement to cut real wages as a restorative to international competitiveness in the early 1950s. Then, when that experience ran into difficulties in the early 1960s, Sweden took over the role of trendsetter. But by the late 1960s that country, too, found its incomes policy disintegrating. Now Norway and Austria are put forward as model countries, particularly the latter since the Norwegians began to disagree in the late 1970s (Gruen, 1983, pp. 2–3).

The work of Schott (1984, 1985), which has assumed a certain prominence in Australia in recent years, further illustrates the problems associated with cross-country comparisons. Schott compares the economic performance of OECD countries against 'measures' of their relative degree of corporatism for the 1970s. Schott uses growth, inflation, and unemployment rates as economic indicators. A performance is categorized as good if the average inflation rate, for example, for the decade was less than 2 per cent, as medium if in the 2–7 per cent range, and as poor if in excess of 7 per cent. After collecting various sets of data and ascertaining the degree of corporatism of different nations Schott concludes that Japan, Austria, Switzerland, and Norway, which are described as strongly corporatist, and the Federal Republic of Germany, a medium corporatist nation, have superior economic performances than do other weak or non-corporatist OECD countries (Schott, 1985, pp. 20–1).

Schott's analysis suffers from both statistical and conceptual problems. If we look at statistical, or data, problems first, Schott claims, by way of example, that Japan, Austria, Germany, and Switzerland experienced (good) average inflation rates of less than 2 per cent in the 1970s, and Norway (medium) in the range 2–7 per cent (Schott, 1985, p. 20). However, data provided by Bruno and Sachs (1985, p. 157) for the same period show that all of the so-called corporatist countries performed less well, against the inflation measure, than Schott suggests. Japan and Norway had (poor) average inflation rates of more than 7 per cent, with Austria, Germany, and Sweden (medium) in the 2–7 per cent range.

The conceptual problems relate to Schott's corporatism classifications, in particular the classifications for Japan, Germany, and Switzerland. It is difficult to see how Japan, with its decentralized, enterprise-based system of industrial relations, and eschewing of incomes policies, could be regarded as a strong corporatist nation.[5] Moreover, how and in what way are Japanese unions incorporated into national economic decision making? It is also difficult to agree with Schott's contention that Germany is medium corporatist.[6] Notwithstanding the existence of industry-level bargaining West Germany does not appear to have pursued incomes policies. Jacobi has pointed out that in West Germany 'the demand for tripartite corporatist arrangements has never been particularly strong' (1985, p. 245). Fuerstenberg has observed that West German governments have adopted the principle of 'bargaining autonomy' and that 'concerted action aiming at a kind of national incomes policy has failed' (1987, pp. 167, 172). Finally, Markovits and Allen have noted that in the 1970s the West German government used monetarist policies and unemployment to combat inflation (1984, p. 141). Schott's claim that Switzerland is a strong corporatist society is based on an article by Kriesi (1982).[7] However, upon reading this article it is somewhat disturbing to discover that Kriesi has in fact said that

Switzerland has virtually no centralised bargaining between capital and labour, and incomes policy in Switzerland is almost non-existent:[8] wage-bargaining is highly decentralised as a result of political and cultural fragmentation [and that Switzerland is not] a good case for corporatism (Kriesi, 1982, pp. 134, 157).

The major problem with determining whether corporatist countries produce economic performances superior to those of non-corporatist countries is empirical: how may different degrees or levels of corporatism can be identified and distinguished? The exercise is highly subjective. For example, while several writers have depicted Australia as having low levels of corporatism, it is apparent that at least in terms of the Bruno and Sachs index Australia would achieve a high score. Notwithstanding the fact that Australia can be reclassified as a highly corporatist nation its economic performance vis-à-vis other OECD countries has been relatively poor. On the other hand, if the above analysis, which rejected Schott's classification of Japan, Switzerland, and West Germany is acceptable, nations with low or minimal levels of corporatism are able to perform well economically. In short, it is difficult to reach a firm conclusion concerning the relative economic performance of corporatist, less corporatist, or non-corporatist countries. The implication of this is that the Accord rests on shaky foundations.

THE NATIONAL ECONOMIC SUMMIT CONFERENCE

In line with his electoral pledge, Prime Minister Hawke rapidly arranged the National Economic Summit Conference, held at Parliament House, Canberra, from 11 to 14 April 1983. There was some politicking over attendees, but ultimately 117 persons, from either of two categories, attended. The summit received wide media coverage. Of the 117 attendees, 100 were 'Official Participants', comprising representatives from Commonwealth, state, territory, and local governments, the ACTU executive, representatives from various employer, business, and professional groups, and a representative from the Australian Council of Social Services. Senator Susan Ryan, in her capacity as a Commonwealth government minister, was the only female 'Official Participant'. The remaining seventeen attendees were afforded 'Observer' status and comprised a rag-bag of representatives from church, women's, ethnic, Aboriginal, financial, consumer, conservation, and professional groups.

In his opening address to the summit the Prime Minister said, 'This is an historic conference — historic not only in the sense that nothing of this scale and scope has been attempted before, but as an event of genuine and seminal importance in the life and history of our country' (Summit, 1983, p. 3). Hawke does not appear to have been aware that the Liberal prime minister Robert Menzies had held a similar two-day conference in Sydney in July 1951, selling a tough, Keynesian budget — what became known as the 1951 'Horror budget' — to overcome the inflationary effects of the Korean war boom (Dabscheck, 1984).

Hawke's opening address is replete with corporatism rhetoric: the need to replace confrontation with consensus, the need for a 'sustained, concerted national effort' — in pursuit of the common goals of economic growth and reconstruction. The tasks of the summit were, according to Hawke

to secure broad agreement on the role of an incomes and prices policy, in our efforts to promote employment and to achieve recovery and growth; and to ensure that the benefits of recovery are not lost in another round of the wages—prices spiral;
to devise machinery for achieving the necessary restraint, including methods of wage fixation, influencing non-wage incomes, and prices surveillance;

to secure a better and wider understanding of the broad economic framework, within which we have to operate;

to seek broad agreement on the relationship between a successful prices and incomes policy and the implementation of policies on industrial relations, job creation and training, taxation, social security, health, education and the other major community services;

to examine the competitiveness and efficiency of the Australian economy;

and finally, to reach agreement on arrangements and machinery to monitor and continue the work of this Conference, especially in regard to continuing the process of consultation and co-operation between government, business, and unions, initiated by this Conference itself (Summit, 1983, p. 3).

Including Hawke's opening address (and excluding his role in the chair) a total of 98 speeches were delivered at the summit. A breakdown of the speeches heard over the four days reveals that 9 were delivered in the afternoon session of day one, 28 on day two, 33 on day three, and 28 on day four. With the possible exception of day one, most speeches were short; Hawke in fact asked speakers to confine their contributions to about ten minutes (Summit, 1983, p. 74). While a number of discussion and information papers were circulated, it is difficult to develop detailed or sophisticated ideas in a short speech. The various speeches at the summit fell into one of the following three categories (with allowances for some overlap). The first category comprised those that were strong on rhetoric, emphasizing the need for consensus and co-operation in these troubled economic times, with attendant congratulations to Hawke for holding the summit. The second category comprised the speakers who basically sought to protect their own bailiwick, indicating how important, indeed crucial, the particular group, organization, or sector had been and/or would continue to be in the achievement of economic growth for Australia. The third category comprised the speakers who identified their organizations' position on particular policy issues, such as whether they were for or against a return to wage indexation.

One of the more interesting aspects of the summit was the manner in which the Hawke government handled its relationship with the employer/business sector. In the discussion which follows it should be remembered that the apparent objective of the summit was to introduce a corporatist, consensus-based incomes policy, following the earlier negotiation of the Accord between the ALP and the ACTU. As the discussion in chapter 1 revealed, a key assumption of corporatism is that employers/business/capital speak with a single voice in helping to bring about the attainment of the common good. The CAI, which in 1977 had become the single, peak federal-level body in Australia, viewed the summit as a chance 'to consolidate its position within the business community' (McEachern, 1986, p. 20); five CAI representatives attended the summit. However, rather than recognize the CAI as the sole voice for the employer/business sector — a recognition afforded the ACTU by its constituency — Hawke decided to invite a further seventeen representatives from various industry-based organizations, eighteen captains of industry, and representatives from three professional groups. The various representatives of employers/business/capital at the summit expressed different views on a wide range of issues; regarding wage determination, for example, some argued for decentralization, others for a continuation of the wages pause well into 1984, others for a centralized system based on productivity, and others for a return to wage indexation.

As noted in Chapters 1 and 2, it should not be surprising that employers/business/capital find it difficult to develop a unified approach. Australian history is replete with examples of rivalry between farming and manufacturing interests. Different firms and enterprises compete with each other across labour, product, and money markets. Any firm competes with suppliers and customers over price and with financial institutions over the cost of capital. Given the diversity and competitive nature of business Hawke's summit invitations may have been appropriate. However, if he seriously wished to take Australia down the corporatist road, Hawke should have recognized the CAI as the sole voice for the employer/business world. Perhaps he decided on the divide-and-rule tactic, making it difficult for employers/business to resist the combined pressure from the Hawke government and the ACTU to have summit endorsement of the essential features of the Accord.

A 56-point communiqué was endorsed by all participants at the summit except Queensland's Premier, Sir Joh Bjelke-Petersen. The communique acknowledged the seriousness of the problems facing the Australian economy and that consensus-based incomes policies were the best means of achieving economic and employment growth. Clause 6 of the communiqué states that in trying to achieve these goals it is important 'to place . . . a restraint on self-interest'. The next two clauses, however, seem to contradict this: 'however, the basic tenets to which all Australians aspire remain fundamentally unaltered' (clause 7); 'it is a legitimate expectation that income of the employed shall be increased in real terms through time in line with productivity' (clause 8) (Summit, 1983, p. 196). The self-restraint inherent in the summit's response to Australia's worst economic crisis in fifty years enshrined the principle of increasing real income over time.

The communiqué is strong on rhetoric, establishing goals, recognizing the need to initiate action on behalf of the more needy and disadvantaged, and proposing the introduction of a wide range of programmes to achieve these equity goals consistent with the need for economic growth and recovery. Apart from its general espousal of the efficacy of incomes policies the communiqué is vague, or silent, on how goals are to be achieved, and on allocation of resources to the various, competing programmes and actions. In the desire to maintain the consensus momentum it was much easier to talk about goals and objectives than ways and means.

The communiqué sought to avoid making hard or contentious decisions. For example, it made no attempt to reach a final decision on the future course of wage determination. While the communiqué endorsed support for a centralized system (clause 20), it decided to leave the issue of how such a system would work to the commission (clauses 21–3). Other notable features of the communiqué were an agreement to establish a prices surveillance body (clauses 25–7) and the creation of an Economic Planning Advisory Council 'to continue the process of consultation' begun at the summit (clause 53).

There are several ways in which the summit can be evaluated. It could be simply viewed as a celebratory event for the new prime minister. Alternatively it could be seen as an 'efficient' means of establishing relations between a new government and representatives of major elites and interest groups. Rather than line up interminable meetings between ministers and leaders to provide appropriate reassurances to each other, why not achieve the same result over a four-day conference? The summit did help to reduce powerful interest groups' uncertainly in the early days of a new federal Labor ministry. Kemp has argued that

In evaluating the summit on its own terms, the question arises whether unnecessary conflict between the major economic interests and between these and government is a major source of Australia's economic problems. An alternative perspective might be that the problem is too much cooperation, and that the political interests of the great economic 'partners' are not identical to the interests of the mass of individuals not represented at the summit (Kemp, 1983, p. 213).

It should also be remembered that the summit was designed to rope in various interest groups, particularly the employer/business sector, to accept or, at a minimum, not oppose the logic of the Accord. While the Accord champions tripartite consensus as the path to economic progress, it should not be forgotten that the Accord was an agreement negotiated between a Hawke-led ALP and the ACTU; the employer/business sector played no part in drawing up the Accord. If Hawke wished to continue the momentum of consensus, upon which he based his political future, he needed to obtain employers/business support for or acquiescence in the Accord. By inviting numerous employer and business representatives and making use of the tactic of divide and rule, by ensuring that the summit communiqué was strong on rhetoric and vague on ways and means, and by delegating 'hard' decisions to other bodies or setting them aside for later consideration Hawke minimized potential opposition. In addition, the sense of occasion (even theatre) and the general consensus euphoria may have induced waiverers to mute the misgivings they may have had concerning the summit communiqué. Sir Peter Abeles, a business representative on the communiqué committee, in what may ultimately be regarded as the quote of the summit, indicated that business and employer representatives

had been out-manoeuvred by the combined forces of the Hawke
government and the ACTU:

> it would only be an extension of the spirit of this Summit if business
> were incorporated as the third party of this accord, as an equal partner
> ... as most of us [employer/business representatives] felt during the
> early days of this Conference, as though we had been invited to play
> singles tennis against a championship doubles combination (Summit,
> 1983, p. 194).

POST-SUMMIT DEVELOPMENTS

This section examines three of the more interesting developments from the summit — the determination of the future course
of wage determination by the commission, and the creation and
roles of the Prices Surveillance Authority and the Economic
Planning Advisory Council.

Soon after the summit the president of the Conciliation and
Arbitration Commission, Sir John Moore, held a series of conferences in an attempt to arrive at consensus concerning the
future direction of wage determination. While the April, May,
and June 1983 conferences revealed that there was general agreement among the parties concerning the need for a centralized
system, there were differences over how such a system should
operate. It was ultimately decided that the commission should
convene a national wage case to resolve the differences. The
ACTU sought a return to automatic, quarterly cost of living
adjustments and a 4.3 per cent increase to wages to compensate
for movements in the consumer price index for the March and
June 1983 quarters. The Commonwealth government argued for
six-monthly rather than quarterly indexation. The CAI argued
for an extension of the wages pause, and maintained that no
increases should be granted until after a review of the economy,
to begin in February 1984.

The commission decided to grant the ACTU's claim for a 4.3
per cent wage increase and to reintroduce a centralized system
based on six-monthly wage indexation, quoting extensively from
both the Accord and the summit in arriving at its decision (NWC,
23 September 1983, pp. 7–11). The principles governing this
new system of wage determination were very similar to those

that had been developed by the commission in the period 1975−81. National wage cases were to be the major source of wage movements, with such increases again being based on the prices plus productivity formula. The commission specified, however, that it would not entertain hearing a productivity claim until 1985. The commission stated that

Increases outside national wage [cases] — whether in the form of wages, allowances or conditions, whether they occur in the public or private sector, whether they be award or overaward — must constitute a very small addition to overall labour costs (NWC, 23 September 1983, p. 49).

Exceptions for wage increases outside national wage cases were the traditional ones of work value, anomalies, and inequities. A new feature associated with these September 1983 principles was that individual unions were required to give an undertaking, before receiving a national wage case increase, that they would 'not pursue any extra claims, award or overaward, except in compliance with the Principles' (NWC, 23 September 1983, p. 49).

The Prices Surveillance Authority (PSA) was established in March 1984, almost a year after the summit. While it has conducted several inquiries (ACPI, 1987), its role and its significance have been relatively minor. Notwithstanding the Accord's and the summit's recommending a fully fledged prices and incomes policy to bring about economic recovery, the actual or major practice of corporatist policy in Australia following the election of the Hawke government in 1983 was confined to the reintroduction of wage indexation. The PSA was created mainly to appease the radical and left-wing elements within unions and the ALP who insisted that if wages were to be controlled by the commission, there should be similar controls on prices. The Hawke government has never been seriously interested in price control or surveillance because of fears that this would lead to a decline in business confidence, which is seen as crucial to the achievement of economic recovery.

The major idea underlying the creation of the Economic Planning Advisory Council (EPAC) was to continue the process of consultation and consensus that had apparently been established at the summit. Formed in 1983, EPAC comprises representatives of Commonwealth and state governments, the ACTU, business/employer organizations, and consumer and welfare groups. Singleton's analysis of EPAC suggests that its actual operation has been substantially less than that which was envisaged or hoped for at the summit. Singleton found that meetings were usually dominated by Commonwealth government ministers and that there was limited time for discussion and debate. In concluding her evaluation of EPAC's role Singleton has said:

> The consensus obtained by EPAC is a long way from the notion of a bargained, negotiated agreement, a collaboration among the groups and between government and the groups, of self-subordination of special interests suggested by the corporatist model. The Hawke-style consensus is about persuasion and co-option, the amelioration of potential conflict with the business sector. It is concerned with the mobilization of consent for government policy. It represents the symbol of participation, not the substance ... Consensus in terms of broad-based community participation, input into policy formulation and true belief in the agreements reached by EPAC is a misnomer, an illusion. EPAC has been used by the government as a facilitator to ease the passage and implementation of policies based on the Accord, to gain the consent and co-operation of powerful sectional groups not party to the Accord (Singleton, 1985, pp. 23–4).

WAGE INDEXATION: A CRITIQUE

Wage indexation was the basis of Australian wage determination in the period 1975–81 and was reintroduced in September 1983 (lasting until mid-1986). The major argument advanced in support of wage indexation is that a centralized system of wage determination achieves superior economic results than, other things being equal, decentralized systems. For example, in reintroducing wage indexation in its September 1983 decision the commission claimed that wage indexation 'offers the best prospects for industrial stability and economic recovery' (NWC, 23 September 1983, p. 48).

The major drawback of decentralized wage determination, according to wage indexation supporters, in the so-called problem associated with the principle of comparative wage justice. For example, Isaac, a former deputy president of the commission and a leading apostle, if not architect, of wage indexation, has claimed that

It is evident from Australian experience that comparative wage justice, backed by industrial pressure, has the potential for damaging economic effects not so much from a relatively rigid structure as from an uncomfortably large rate of increase in the general wage level ... By recognising comparative wage justice as a force to be accommodated by national wage adjustments but severely limiting its influence in other adjustments, a centralised system of wage fixing [where wage rises are linked to movements in prices] provides an opportunity to minimise economic damage both directly and through industrial disputes' (Isaac, 1986, p. 103).

Five criticisms may be levelled at Isaac's claims concerning wage indexation and comparative wage justice.

1 the definition of comparative wage justice
2 evidence, or rather the lack of evidence, concerning the pressures of comparative wage justice on the process of wage determination
3 whether centralized wages policies increase or decrease comparative wage justice pressures
4 how centralized wages policies based on indexation reduce the length of lags and/or speed up the adjustment process
5 the demise of the metal trades as Australia's traditional wage leader.

What does the term *comparative wage justice* mean? While it is part and parcel of the jargon of Australian industrial relations, it is used imprecisely and has become a catch-all phrase, meaning all things to all persons. Isaac (1986, pp. 85−6) claims that the origins of the term can be traced to a decision of the South Australian Industrial Court by Thomas Hewitson (9 SAIR 167, pp. 184−5), a member of the Court between 1923 and 1930 and president from 1927 to 1930. However, Hewitson's predecessor, William Jethro Brown, president of the Court from 1916 to 1927, had earlier developed the term 'comparable wages' in the 1921 *Trading Banks Clerks* case. In that case Jethro Brown said 'comparable wages ... requires a reference to the wages in as large a number of industries comparable to the industry in question' (4 SAIR 181, p. 211). In earlier cases Jethro Brown had made use of such terms as 'comparative efficiency' (2 SAIR 31, p. 41), 'comparable occupations' (2 SAIR 267, p. 271), and 'the comparative method' (3 SAIR 11, p. 23).

It is possible to develop a spectrum or typology of definitions of comparative wage justice on examination of interpretations by the commission and its predecessor the Court. Rudimentary, simple, advanced, and sophisticated forms of comparative wage justice have been considered.

Rudimentary comparative wage justice operates when a tribunal decides that all workers under its jurisdiction should receive wage increases of virtually the same amount, or percentage, at exactly the same, specified time. Uniform increases will be granted notwithstanding differences in the skill, occupation, or industry of employees, the economic health or well-being of employers, a short supply or an over-supply of labour, the degree or nature of technological change, labour—capital ratios, when wage increases where last granted, and so on. National wage cases are the vehicle for rudimentary comparative wage justice increases. Isaac, in discussing the role of national wage cases and comparative wage justice, has said:

> the transmission of a wage increase generally, almost simultaneously on a test case procedure, effectively recognised the merit of a general flow-on and so avoided the need for claims invoking comparative wage justice to be argued award by award as was necessary in earlier times. Implicitly ... total wage increases[9] should therefore be regarded as based on an application of comparative wage justice or, more accurately, on comparative wage increase justice ... the practice of national wage adjustments may be seen as the logical development of institutionalised comparative wage justice (Isaac, 1986, pp. 89—95).

This quote from Isaac is confusing and contradictory. While saying that national wage cases avoid 'the need for claims invoking comparative wage justice', Isaac says that national wage cases are 'based on an application of comparative wage justice or, more accurately, on comparative wage increase justice'; national wage cases, which, according to Isaac, overcome the problem of comparative wage justice, are nonetheless based on that principle. National wage cases grant all workers a synchronized wage increase, whereas the comparative wage justice *principle* rests on case-by-case determination of wage increases. With reference to Isaac it would seem that national wage cases, especially based on wage indexation, where the commission seeks to confine wage increases from other sources to a minimum, rather than removing or overcoming comparative wage justice pressures, represent a total capitulation to that principle.

Simple comparative wage justice refers to a situation where a tribunal increases the wages of workers because other workers have gained increases or because there have been movements in average wages. No attempt is made to examine the nature of the work performed by the different groups of workers concerned. Increases in wages gained elsewhere simply provide the justification for increasing the wages of other workers who have not gained similar increases. Simple comparative wage justice is an important mechanism through which wage increases are transmitted in the Australian system of wage determination. Isaac has pointed out that 'It is likely that the application by tribunals of [comparative wage justice] . . . may have raised the rate of weaker sections of the workforce above the rate which would have otherwise prevailed' (1986, p. 95).

Advanced comparative wage justice occurs when a tribunal makes comparisons with workers performing similar work; the nature of the work itself provides the basis of comparisons. The view 'that employees doing the same work for different employers or in different industries should by and large receive the same amount of pay irrespective of the capacity of their employer or industry' (134 CAR 159, p. 165) predicates these comparisons. However, it has never been clear why, just because one group of workers gained a wage increase, this should justify an increase to other workers doing the 'same' work with other employers or in another industry. Generally, tribunals have required the parties desirous of an increase to prove that the work, in its relevant characteristics, in the two situations, is the same or that the circumstances warranting an increase in the first instance also apply to the second group of workers.

Sophisticated comparative wage justice refers to attempts by a tribunal to order different work and occupations into a hierarchy and simultaneously to ensure that the relative wages of the workers concerned match this hierarchy. As Provis has said:

comparative wage justice can be taken to imply not only that equal pay should be given to people who do the same work, but also that there should be an appropriate ratio between people's pay when they do different work, a ratio determined by the difference in the jobs (Provis, 1986, p. 27).

In determining or altering a particular wage the tribunal attempts to determine a wage which will be regarded as being fair, just, and equitable, in the context of a series of wages, if not all wages. For example, in the 1954 *Metal Trades Margins* case the Arbitration Court declared that

the assessment of each margin[10] should be made in relation to each other margin, so that the margin awarded to one employee should bear, as far as possible, its proper monetary comparison with that of every other employee awarded a margin, having in mind the various matters which in each case should be weighted in assessing the margin (80 CAR 3, p. 24).

There is also evidence of there being problems with the impact of comparative wage justice on the process of wage determination. There are two well-known facts concerning Australian wages. The first concerns the use of incremental scales, or wage ladders, which are a prominent feature of public sector and white collar employment. In these areas of the labour market, job classifications include a series of scales or increments identifying different wage levels. Generally, the employees concerned receive a pay increment each year, over and above increases in award wages. Notwithstanding the fact that the workers concerned are doing the same work, and have the same job classification, they receive different rates of pay, keyed to seniority. In both public sector and white collar employment, seniority is an important factor which significantly modifies the force of comparative wage justice.

The second fact about Australian wages is that over-award pay and special payments such as site allowances are a pervasive feature of, especially, blue collar employment in Australia. Over-award pay and special payments vary over time and between and across industries (Gill, 1985; Kyloh, 1985; Zeremes, 1985). Clearly workers performing the same job in the same and/or different industries receive different levels of remuneration.

Centralized systems of wage determination imply that the extent, if not timing, of wage increases and/or improvements to conditions should be the same or similar for all workers. The problem with this, and it is a problem of wage and incomes policies generally, is that if a group of workers gains a wage increase, or any other concession over and above the 'dictates' of the centralized system, other, if not all, workers will mount pressures for similar increases. The 1978 $8 work-value round, the reduced-hours campaign in the early 1980s, and the super-annuation claim in the mid-1980s (see Chapter 5) are demonstrations of this. In a very real sense centralized wages policies are in a perpetual state of crisis, because exceptional treatment, for whatever reason, threatens the centralized system's rationale and continued operation.[11]

Wage rises, or wage-rounds, take time to flow through an economy under decentralized systems of wage determination. However, the inference from this statement should not be that such flows are determined by (simple) comparative wage justice pressures. Subject to the policy stance adopted by the commission, the extent and timing of such flows would be determined by the myriad economic forces (broadly defined) relevant to the respective groups of concerned parties. The problem of a centralized system of wage determination where wage increases are uniformly synchronized for all workers is that the length of wage-rounds is reduced — or lags are eliminated — or the adjustment process within the economy is speeded up. Prior to the introduction of wage indexation Boehm (1974) estimated that the duration of lags associated with wage-rounds ranged from three years to six months, the length varying inversely with the trade cycle.

Traditionally, unions in the metal trades have been regarded as the wage leaders in Australia. Metal unions have historically been militant and at the forefront of major campaigns and struggles for improvements in wages and working conditions (Sheridan, 1975). Since the early 1970s, however, the manufacturing sector has been in decline, which in turn has blunted the ability of metal workers to gain concessions (the negotiation of a 38-hour standard working week during the short-lived mining and resources boom of 1981—82 being a notable exception). Boehm's study of wage-rounds noted that the metal trades award had been converted from a wage leader to a wage follower (Boehm, 1974, pp. 42—4). More significantly, Richardson's (1982) study of metal workers in the 1970s found that their earnings had fallen behind movements in average weekly earnings.

CONCLUSION

Prior to the March 1983 general election the ALP and the ACTU negotiated an Accord which committed both to a series of undertakings if and when the ALP assumed electoral office. For its part the ALP would initiate a number of social reforms and it agreed with the ACTU that real wages should be maintained over time. In the context of Australia's worst economic crisis since the Depression of the 1930s the Accord rested on the assumption that economic recovery would be achieved by the commission's reintroduction of wage indexation.

The new prime minister had based his campaign on the link between a corporatist, consensus-based incomes policy and economic growth and progress. The National Economic Summit Conference which Prime Minister Hawke convened within weeks of his electoral victory created the impression that critical sections of Australian society, particularly the employer/business sector, endorsed or, at a minimum, did not oppose the Accord. In September 1983 the Conciliation and Arbitration Commission brought a new system of wage indexation into being. The system was opposed by the Confederation of Australian Industry.

The major result of the election of the Hawke government was to convert the wages freeze to a system of wage indexation. Assuming that the commission wished to reintroduce wage indexation (see Chapter 2) the ALP (and the ACTU), realizing this, gained political kudos and power from appearing to be responsible for its implementation.

Two of the major ideas underpinning the Accord — that corporatist societies have economic performances superior to non-corporatist societies, and the usefulness of wage indexation as a means of achieving economic recovery — have been challenged in this chapter. The major problem in deciding on superiority of economic performance is finding an appropriate index or measure to ascertain whether and to what degree a particular society is corporatist. More generally, the chapter has revealed the difficulties associated with the transformation of an abstract theoretical concept, such as corporatism, into a usable empirical construct. To talk about different Western-style capitalist democracies as having strong, medium, or weak corporatist characteristics seems to make nonsense of theoretical discussions of corporatism, which are based on notions of strict, centralized controls imposed at the national level. What does it mean to describe a society as being medium corporatist? Does it mean that the society is half corporatist and half (societal) pluralist? How can that society be corporatist and pluralist at the same time? Criticism of wage indexation, the other tenet of the Accord that required examination, was levelled at the operation of so-called comparative wage justice pressures in decentralized systems of wage determination.

The major argument advanced by those who support the Accord is that consensus-based policies are the best way to achieve economic growth and recovery. The effectiveness of the Accord, then, can be tested against economic results. In both 1983 and 1984 the Australian economy experienced recovery. Whether this was due to the Accord or to other factors and whether indeed, in the absence of the Accord, recovery would have been more pronounced, the Accord partners, particularly the Hawke government, were able to take credit. However, during the second half of 1985 and in 1986 the economy experienced a number of major problems, particularly with respect to the international sector, which placed the Accord under extreme pressure.

Before we consider Accord developments of the second half of the 1980s, however, the issue of industrial relations reform and the Hancock Report will be examined.

NOTES

1 For further details of Hawke's career and his attainment of the office of Prime Minister see d'Alpuget (1982), Hurst (1983), and Kelly (1984).

2 Chapter 2 showed that the ACTU did not oppose the wages freeze when it was introduced by the commission on 23 December 1982.

3 The basic thrust of the ideas contained in this paragraph was confirmed in a conversation with Sir John Moore on 5 November 1987 at the University of New South Wales.

4 See Schott (1984, 1985), Bruno and Sachs (1985), and Tarantelli (1986). For criticisms of this view see Addison (1984).

5 Bruno and Sachs (1985, p. 241) describe Japan as medium corporatist.

6 Bruno and Sachs consider Germany to be highly corporatist.

7 Bruno and Sachs describe Switzerland as medium corporatist, and Tarantelli (1986) does not even include it in his analysis, where he argues that corporatist nations economically out-perform non-corporatist nations.

8 This point has also been noted by von Beyme (1980, p. 272).

9 i.e. national wage cases.

10 Before the introduction of the total wage in 1967, Australia, at the federal level, had a dual, or bifurcated, system of wages. The basic wage was a minimum wage determined in accordance with the needs of the worker and the capacity of the economy to pay. Margins were an extra wage to compensate workers for the extra skill or responsibility that their work entailed.

11 The 1946—47 metal trades industry dispute and subsequent wage increases brought an end to the Chifley Labor government's post—World War II wage controls. See Sheridan (1973, 1975, 1986).

CHAPTER 4

Industrial Relations Reform

The Accord contained a statement which committed an Australian Labor Party government to establishing

in consultation with the [Australian Council of Trade Unions] and employers, an Inquiry into the Conciliation and Arbitration Act and Regulations to conduct a total review of federal industrial legislation to improve that legislation. Within the review, priority consideration should be given to reform the laws relating to the internal affairs of unions to ensure the continued effective, efficient and democratic operation of unions (Accord, p. 8).

Clause 34 of the National Economic Summit Conference communiqué included a statement that 'the Government will initiate a fundamental review of the Conciliation and Arbitration Act and Regulations aimed at improving legislation in the area of industrial relations' (Summit, 1983, p. 198).

On 14 July 1983 Ralph Willis, the Minister for Employment and Industrial Relations, announced the establishment of the Committee of Review into Australian Industrial Relations Law and Systems. The three people constituting the committee were Professor Keith Hancock, vice-chancellor of Flinders University, as chairperson; Charlie Fitzgibbon, former senior vice-president of the Australian Council of Trade Unions; and George Polites, former director-general of the Confederation of Australian Industry. The committee had these terms of reference:

With the aim and for the purpose of developing a more effective and practical industrial relations system in accordance with social, economic and industrial changes which have occurred and are taking place in Australia, there [shall] be established a Committee of Review to examine, report and make recommendations not later than 31 March 1985, on:
(a) all aspects of Commonwealth law relating to the prevention and settlement of industrial disputes;

(b) all aspects of Commonwealth law relating to the recognition and operation of associations of employers and workers;

(c) the extent to which and the manner in which the Federal and State industrial relations institutional and legislative arrangements might better inter-relate (Hancock Report, pp. 1−2).

The Hancock Report, as the deliberations of the committee of review became known, was handed down on 30 April 1985.

This chapter provides a critical examination of the Hancock Report. Firstly, however, the term *reform* in the industrial relations context requires attention.

DEFINING INDUSTRIAL RELATIONS REFORM

Different groups and organizations have different viewpoints and ideas as to the best or most desirable industrial relations approach or method. Each organization would like to have its own industrial relations 'heaven'. A problem that all organizations encounter in pursuing their unique goals and objectives is convincing other organizations of the wisdom of adopting their particular plan of action; all organizations are constrained by the different goals, objectives, and powers of those they relate to and interact with.

In seeking to realize their goals organizations will develop tactics and strategies in an attempt to convince or convert other organizations with whom they interact. One strategy is to claim that one's goals embody 'reform'. Since the word has been pushed to generic status, opposition to 'reform' is, for some, synonymous with opposition to 'progress'. Claiming that a desired goal or objective is a 'reform' allows criticisms to be countered on the basis of being 'anti-reform' and, by implication, not worthy of consideration or any serious analysis.

The problem remains, however, of defining the term. One approach is to define reform in terms of a change that one approves of or likes. The difficulty with this is that in real-world industrial relations, replete with conflict, what is regarded as desirable by some is invariably opposed and/or rejected by others.

We will therefore define *industrial relations reform* as a change in procedural rules, that is, those rules which determine or define the way in which the various organizations involved in industrial relations interact. The roots of this definition can be found in the work of Dunlop (1958) (see Chapter 1). Organizations can have strongly held and opposing views of the desirability or otherwise of any set of procedural rules, so we are not defining reform in terms of whether organizations *like* the changes in procedural rules. Rather, all changes in procedural rules are regarded as constituting reform — and we are managing to neutralize the word as well. Reform, or a change in procedural rules, is part and parcel of the clash of ideas and struggles which pervade real-world industrial relations.

Changes in procedural rules can result from decisions of unions and employers as they find different ways to interact, from the legislative changes of governments, from the decisions of the High Court as it defines the rights and obligations of parties and continually determines federal and state boundaries, and from various decisions of the industrial tribunals in Australia. It might be useful, in fact, to regard the various industrial tribunals as constituting a group of quasi-royal commissions charged with the responsibility of drawing to the attention of the parties, governments, and the general public various proposals concerning the reform of industrial relations. Reform, or a change in procedural rules, is, then, continually occurring in Australian industrial relations.

THE HANCOCK REPORT

It might be useful at this point to highlight a key difference between the methodological approach employed by the Hancock Report and the approach used by the (British) Royal Commission on Trade Unions and Employers Associations (the Donovan Report) and the task force on Canadian industrial relations (the Canadian Report), both of which reported in 1968. In both Britain and Canada fairly extensive research programmes were conducted or commissioned to determine the conduct and operation of industrial relations (Donovan Report, p. 337; Canadian Report, pp. 240–50). The Hancock Report, however, decided against initiating or undertaking research into the operation of Australian industrial relations. While the committee employed two consultants, who conducted original research — on federal and state unions in Western Australia; the role of internal and external influences upon the industrial relations practices of organizations — incorporation of the results of these studies is not indicated in the report.[1]

The Hancock Report includes information and material from four basic sources:[2]

1 The submissions of interested parties (a total of 154 were received)
2 The Accord, the summit proceedings, and the wage indexation decisions of the Australian Conciliation and Arbitration Commission
3 Legal counsel on particular questions of law
4 Especially with respect to the fine print of various sections of the Conciliation and Arbitration Act, the Searby and Taylor Report (1981).

The report does not include research material devoted to Australian industrial relations other than at Chapter 4 and Appendix II, both of which examine wage issues, an area which has been a continuing research interest of Professor Hancock.

Australian industrial relations research in last decade has undergone an important transformation, even a golden age. In the last decade, publications have included three textbooks, collected readings, the proceedings of conferences, and topical monographs based on long-term research. The Industrial Relations Research Centre and the National Institute of Labour Studies have been actively involved in the production and dissemination of industrial relations information.[3] There is also the steady stream of research and information published by the *Journal of Industrial Relations* and the *Australian Bulletin of Labour* and included in the articles that appear in the wide range of legal journals.

The committee, however, in a 694-page report and 245 pages of appendixes refers to only twelve articles from the *Journal of Industrial Relations*, two from the *Australian Bulletin of Labour*, three publications from both the National Institute of Labour Studies and the Industrial Relations Research Centre, and eleven legal publications (which is particularly noteworthy given the terms of reference and the inclusion of 'law' in the committee's title). It is somewhat ironic that the Hancock Report endorses 'the need for a higher priority to be given to industrial relations research' (III, p. 49).

The committee waited for interested parties to offer submissions. Although a series of public hearings were held, the committee did not, other than by its terms of reference, indicate to parties the types of issues and questions on which it would like to receive submissions. The only exception was a request to the Department of Employment and Industrial Relations to provide additional information in a second submission. This ad hoc approach may be contrasted with that of the Donovan Commission, which, by the end of the third month of its commission, had circulated a list of 330 questions by which it sought to direct interested parties in preparation of their submissions (Donovan Report, pp. 308−18).

The Hancock Report relies heavily on Sir John Moore's 26-page submission as well as the Accord, the summit proceedings, and the wage indexation decisions of the commission. The report has consequently been criticized for celebrating the status quo: if the Accord, the summit, and wage indexation were the solutions for the problems of industrial relations regulation and economic recovery, why conduct a review? The 1981 Searby and Taylor Report could have served as an appropriate basis for revision and redrafting of the Conciliation and Arbitration Act. A further reason for the Hancock Report being so anticlimactic was that either the committee could not identify the significant problems requiring solutions, or the problems it highlights are more imagined than real.

Finally, and this is a particularly disturbing point, where the Hancock Report has asked senior legal counsel for opinions on certain legal issues, it has reported their answers only in terms of yes or no, such a power is available, or such a procedure would survive High Court scrutiny. For reasons which are not at all clear the Hancock Report does not incorporate, even in appendix form, the reasoning or basis for those decisions. It is difficult to begin to check or evaluate the opinions of the legal counsel.

The Hancock Report is poorly structured. It seems to comprise three reports rather than one: first, a textbook (Chapters 2 and 3 in particular, and the general provision of information in other chapters); second, a defence of wages policy (Chapter 4 especially and Chapter 5); third, an industrial relations report. Also the report suffers from poor organization of its material. It is surprising that Chapter 4, devoted to the advocacy of wages policy, should appear before Chapter 5, The Choice of an Industrial Relations System. The latter, more fundamental issue, given the terms of reference, should have been canvassed first. Also, important sections of Chapter 10 — specifically those concerned with the choice between or the mix of conciliation and arbitration and the role of industry councils — should have been integrated with Chapter 5. By delegating such discussion to the penultimate chapter, the report down-plays the significance of these issues and ignores their potential as bases for alternative industrial relations systems.

Various parts of the Hancock Report are confused or contradictory. On page 531 we are told that there is no voluntary arbitration in Australia, but, at page 635, 'Australia has a de facto voluntary system of arbitration'.

The committee's position on a wage-indexation-based wages policy is far from clear. On page 159 the report rejects the view that wage indexation caused wages to be higher than they would have been in the absence of wage indexation. On page 168 we are told that the committee did not 'wish to be construed as supporting or opposing indexation. Rather, we have attempted in general terms to state the pros and cons'. However, on the very next page they decided to endorse wage indexation after all:

The evidence as to how the Conciliation and Arbitration Commission has affected Australia's experience in respect of inflation and unemployment is less than decisive, but certainly does not support confident assertions about ill-effects due to the Commission's presence and its policies. Many and serious uncertainties beset the suggestion of a permanent abandonment of centralised wage fixation. At this stage, we do not think that the incurring of these uncertainties is warranted; and there are possibilities of the centralised system's contributing significantly to Australia's economic recovery (p. 169).

On page 204, however, the report casts doubt on the value of wage indexation as a means of controlling inflation: 'One mechanism, among others, whereby general inflationary pressures may be transmitted into larger wage increases is the indexation of wages.' Finally, on page 529, in rejecting employer attempts to link wage rises to capacity to pay, international competitiveness, or productivity, the report states: 'It would be unwise ... to link the operation of the system in a specific way to various indicators that have been used from time to time. These reflect economic doctrines that enjoy varying degrees of support and whose prescription might cause inflexibility, and confusion.' It is difficult to square this statement with a policy that supports wage indexation, where wage rises are linked to movements in a macroeconomic indicator, the consumer price index.

The Hancock Report claims on pages 154 and 171 that countries that have adopted 'strongly corporatist' arrangements have performed more ably, showing lower rates of inflation and unemployment. Australia, which uses a conciliation and arbitration system, is described by the report as being weakly corporatist.[4] All the other countries mentioned (members of the Organization for Economic Co-operation and Development (OECD)[5]) are usually described as 'collective bargaining countries' in the Hancock Report's presentation of corporatism.

Putting to one side whether countries such as Switzerland, Germany, and Japan can be usefully regarded as corporatist — a proposition which we rejected in Chapter 3 — and whether there is more to corporatism than mere tripartism, it is surprising to read the statement on page 242:[6]

The present system [i.e. Australia's conciliation and arbitration system] affords the mechanism of a wage policy. This, we believe, is a useful instrument of economic policy, particularly for the pursuit of macroeconomic objectives. Although an alternative industrial relations system might accommodate a wage policy, we cannot be confident that it would do so.

What has happened to the 'collective bargaining countries', cited earlier as a model for Australia in pursuit of successful corporatist arrangements?

On pages 544–5 the report rejects the claim that arbitration has a deadening effect on negotiations between parties. On page 574, however, in summarizing a Department of Employment and Industrial Relations survey of the use of Boards of Reference, the report says: 'Despite the relatively high incidence of Boards of Reference, our understanding is that the parties to awards make little use of them. There is a strong tendency to go direct to the Commission when seeking a resolution of a matter arising under the award.'

On page 242 we are told: 'The conciliation and arbitration system is, to a degree, adaptable and can accommodate practices and policies which differ from those now obtaining. Thus, if the parties to industrial relations wish to rely more heavily upon negotiation ... they are free to do so.' This does not sit well with the Hancock Report's general advocacy of a wages policy based on wage indexation; note, for example, page 171:

The indexation system cannot be maintained if wage increases negotiated 'outside the system' become widespread. Should this occur, the Conciliation and Arbitration Commission would no longer be in a position to administer a wage policy and its role would be one of facilitating dispute settlement in a labour market dominated by bargaining power.

Finally, to what extent can overseas experience be used as a guide to policy or projections for Australia? It has already been noted that the Hancock Report expresses enthusiastic support for corporatist policies pursued by OECD collective bargaining countries. When it comes to the issue of union structure, however, the Hancock Report maintains that little can be gained from overseas experience (notwithstanding its advocacy of industry unionism and the abolition of unions with fewer than 1000 members as desirable long-term goals). On pages 459–60 it says: 'we find it unhelpful to be directed to overseas examples where, it is said, a smaller number of unions exist and operate more effectively. Like other elements of the industrial relations system, the structure of trade unions is a product of the environment of the country in which it exists.' The problem for the reader is, how can overseas experience not be a guide on the issue of union structure, yet be a guide when corporatist structures are being advocated?

The report also contains a number of unfounded assertions. One example concerns the claim, made on page 295, that the differences in procedures and legislation of the state and federal systems 'can only confuse and irritate'. No evidence is provided to substantiate this claim. Moreover, while the variety of legislation and procedures may appear baffling to students and the uninitiated, it does not appear to cause problems for the parties. It is interesting to note that the Hancock Report, in following Sir John Moore's submission, on page 512 points out that at the federal level at least 'proceedings before the Commission are remarkably free of legalism'.

On page 334 the Hancock Report refers to the 'external affairs' and 'corporations' powers in the Australian Constitution as being 'exotic'; it exhorts the Commonwealth government not to use these powers to enhance its legislative scope and to rely solely on the use of the 'conciliation and arbitration' power. While the committee's adjective 'exotic' presents only semantic difficulties when applied to powers that have always been available, subject to High Court interpretation, and that are part of the Australian Constitution, there is naïvety in suggesting to Commonwealth governments that they ought not to use available powers to pursue their objectives or enhance their prospects of electoral success. In more than eighty years of Australian history, Commonwealth governments have not been overly worried about increasing their power vis-à-vis the states.

The committee's view of industrial disputation is somewhat truncated. The statement on page 65 that 'perhaps the only measurable dimension of industrial relations "performance" [is] the incidence of stoppages and the loss of working time caused by them'[7] is at odds with the statement on page 123 that 'the cost of lost time due to stoppages is more difficult to absorb than the costs of accidents, illness, absenteeism and labour turnover'. Leaving aside the fact that since 1970 each Australian worker has spent only slightly more than half a day per annum on strike (see Table 6.1), one wonders why the Hancock Report did not refer to the links between levels of productivity, unemployment, under-employment, inflation, the balance of payments, and the exchange rate and industrial relations performance. In any case, production losses caused by factors other than work stoppages — accidents, illness, absenteeism, and labour turnover — can be measured. Crawford and Volard (1981), for example, have shown that the losses from accidents, illness, and absenteeism are each greater than those from industrial disputes. It is estimated that more than 400 Australians are killed at work each year. The measurement of production losses from death and injuries must take account of the extensive production delays that frequently follow, the rebuilding costs that are sometimes incurred, the costly political and judicial inquiries that may be involved, and not least the reparation and compensation claims.

On page 124 the Hancock Report asserts that 'on average, the indirect costs of stoppages exceed the direct costs by a substantial margin'. No information or evidence is provided to support this claim. On pages 616 and 617 the report claims that the effect and implications of demarcation disputes are greater than those indicated by official statistics on industrial disputes, which show that demarcation disputes account for only 1.9 per cent of total working days lost. Again, no evidence is supplied in support of this claim. The committee would have been well advised to examine Wright's (1983, 1984) research into demarcation disputes.

It will by now be clear that the Hancock Report lacks a theoretical base; at best its approach is description as prescription. The report does make three excursions into industrial relations theory, but these result in confusion rather than clarification. On pages 12 and 13 the report seeks to identify a common assumption that binds the parties together, or at least enables them to resolve their differences. This search for a common assumption, or 'ideology', is in the best tradition of Dunlop's (1958) systems model (see Chapter 1). The key passage reads:

The assumption is that while management and unions do not have a commonality of purpose, they have areas of common interest in the preservation of the organisation and its jobs. Perceiving this common interest, the conflicting parties limit their actions accordingly. They . . . do so . . . rather than jeopardise the continuity of the enterprise (pp. 12-13).

The report goes on to describe this as a 'pluralist type of model'. The model, of course, is firm-based and bears a strong resemblance to that developed by Fox (1966, 1973, 1974; see Chapter 1).

A major problem of firm-based models is that they ignore the role of governments,[8] industrial tribunals, and superior courts (more generally, the role of the state), and abstract themselves from the problems of interdependency that exist between various industrial relations (sub)systems. This last point is particularly noteworthy, given the Hancock Report's concern with comparative wage justice and the relationship between state and federal tribunals. Moreover, one of the implications of employing a firm-based model is that industrial relations policies and reforms should logically be directed at the firm level and designed to enhance the development of a decentralized industrial relations system. Such an approach is inconsistent with the report's advocacy of the need for a centralized wages policy.

Also, it is doubtful whether the basic assumption of 'the preservation of the organisation and its jobs' provides an adequate foundation for understanding the dynamics of Australian industrial relations. Fortunately or unfortunately the essential nature of capitalist societies is competitive and conflict-based. New industries and firms emerge to replace those that cannot maintain the pace of competitive life; the aim is to drive one's competitors out of business and reap the benefits of a less competitive and more monopolistic environment. As the Hancock Report itself notes on page 20, fair wages were introduced in Australia to 'restrict the ability of unscrupulous employers to compete in the market, and hence prevent cut-throat competition'. As early as 1909, Mr Justice Higgins declined to alter an award because of the possible threat of closure. On that occasion he said:

It is quite possible that when I give my award some will attribute the stoppage of the mine to the award . . . But if such a statement be made, it will simply by untrue. What stops the mining is the deficiency of payable ore ... I face the possibility of the mine remaining closed, with all its grave consequences; but the fate of Australia is not dependent on the fate of any one mine, or any one Company; and if it is a calamity that this historic mine should close down, it would be a still greater calamity that men should be underfed or degraded (3 CAR 1, pp. 33—4).

Besides, employers introduce technological change and new methods of work organization that frequently result in short- and long-term unemployment. Because of this 'disemployment', state governments have introduced protective legislation, and industrial tribunals have handed down awards determining periods of notice and levels of redundancy pay — in effect making redundancies orderly (or legitimizing them). Could it be argued that the general move to part-time work — examined on pages 71—5 of the report — constitutes an erosion of job rights, and of adult female workers particularly?

With regard to premisses the Hancock Report acknowledges on page 13 that the 'assumption does not always hold good', but adds 'that the assumption is generally right'. The committee would have been well advised to drop the assumption altogether, or to seek an alternative explanation of what motivates the various parties constituting the Australian industrial relations system. An alternative and more suitable model would have rested on the self-interest assumption, with the various parties, including the various organs of the state, being involved in on-going 'competition', or 'bargaining', or 'conflict'.

The Hancock Report sometimes moves away from a firm-based model of industrial relations. On page 633, in examining the issue of unions and sanctions, the report refers to a 'pluralistic society' (see Chapter 1 for a discussion of societal-based pluralist models). As has already been noted, the report is also favourably disposed to the model of 'corporatism', a model which operates at a societal level. The Hancock Report, however, provides no explanation of how it is able to switch either from a firm-based pluralist model to a societal-based pluralist model or between societal pluralist and corporatist models.

One of the weakest sections of the Hancock Report is the treatment, or rather lack of treatment, of alternatives to the present conciliation and arbitration system and structures in Australia. (On page 158 the report does note that the Commonwealth Treasury, a continuing critic of wage indexation during the Fraser years, failed to tender a submission. It should be recalled here that the Commonwealth Department of Employment and Industrial Relations financed and serviced the inquiry, not the Department of the Treasury, and it is therefore likely that a high-level decision was taken to keep the 'voice' of the parliamentary departments to one only.) For reasons which are not made clear, Chapter 5 of the report downplays or ignores many of the alternative proposals suggested to it; slightly more than four pages (pages 215–19) are devoted to the submissions presented on this issue. The report deliberates over collective bargaining and arbitration only (given its advocacy of wages policy in Chapter 4, it is not surprising that the report opted for arbitration). Reference to the numerous and varied types of arbitral/tribunal systems — that is, the different arrangements developed by the states (described in Chapter 3) and the evolution of the federal tribunal (described in Chapter 2) — is absent.

In Chapter 5 there is no attempt to discuss a decentralized tribunal system, which would have required examination of the balance between conciliation and arbitration, the development of wages/industrial boards at the federal level, the use of industry councils, island industries in the style of the Coal Industry Tribunal, and benefits for the federal system by borrowing arrangements and structures that operate in the various state systems (over the years the state and the federal systems have borrowed from each other).

While the roles of conciliation and of industry councils are considered in Chapter 10 of the Hancock Report, these issues are examined in the context of being consistent with the dictates of wages policy. There is no consideration of their potential as alternatives to conciliation and arbitration as they operate at the federal level.

In Chapter 5 the Hancock Report also presents information on a conference the committee sponsored in October 1984 — Alternatives to the Present Arbitration System: Needs, Options and Strategies — where a series of papers were delivered by practitioners, arbitrators, and academics (Blandy and Niland, 1986). The report devotes a total of five pages (pp. 219–24) to the conference, presenting extracts from selected papers, but in examining specific issues, such as the working of particular sections of the Act, only one conference idea — Ludeke's (1986) proposal concerning industry councils — is used. On page 219 the report states that 'The papers presented to the conference will be published by the organisers of the conference,[9] and we do not attempt to deal comprehensively with them'. One wonders of course if the conference should have been held at all if the material that resulted from it was to be of so little use to the committee in its deliberations.

One of the interesting side-shows on publication of the report was the complaint that those who were opposed to the operation of the conciliation and arbitration system did not present submissions.[10] It would be more accurate to say that the problem was not so much that alternative proposals were not submitted but that they were ignored.

Three interesting reform proposals were advocated by the Hancock Report:

1 the dual appointment, or cross-commissioning, of personnel to state and federal tribunals to enhance the attainment of an integrated state and federal system of industrial relations
2 the development of a new tribunal system at the federal level by creating a new court and commission and by the use of dual appointees
3 the abolition of unions with fewer than 1000 members.

The committee was clearly desirous of establishing an integrated system of industrial relations. On page 279 of the report 'a merging of Commonwealth and state industrial tribunals on a "federalist" basis — resulting in the one institution exercising federal and state industrial powers' is posited. Such an objective can apparently be achieved by 'intense and genuine discussion' (p. 285). The report maintains that one of the ways to enhance the attainment of an integrated system is by dual appointment of tribunal members, that is 'the appointment of some members of the state tribunal . . . as members of the federal tribunal and the appointment of some members of the federal tribunal as members of the state tribunal' (recommendation 7 (iii)). On page 292 the virtues of dual appointments are extolled: they 'would be viable and useful in providing more flexibility, enhancing capacity to react promptly to situations and promoting co-ordination between federal and state tribunals'.

Notwithstanding this, the Hancock Report's position on dual appointments is ambiguous if not confused. For example, with respect to section 41(1) (d) matters — where the commission determines whether a matter should be heard by a state or federal tribunal — the Hancock Report, on page 299, rejects dual appointments because 'the decision taking process ... [would] be complicated by the introduction of "independent" or composite federal/state tribunals'. And when it comes to the question of using a dual state appointee to determine whether a worker covered by a federal award should be reinstated — an area where the federal tribunal has traditionally experienced constitutional problems[11] — the Hancock Report states:

Although a person who holds office as both a member of the federal arbitral body and a member of a state arbitral body may be able to call on powers from both jurisdictions to deal with reinstatement cases, we do not regard dual appointments as the solution to the problem. This course would require cross-jurisdictional action, which could be confusing and complex (p. 352).

There may also be administrative problems: what is the jurisdiction of a state-based dual appointee? It is unclear as to whether this person would share powers with the federal dual appointee over matters confined to his or her state, or whether such powers could be extended to determine matters in other states. If the powers of state-based dual appointees include the latter, it is conceivable that an aggrieved party in a second state could take exception to the decisions(s) of another state tribunal and initiate legal or other proceedings to seek redress. One way around this problem could be to have a number of state representatives (if not all) sitting with a federal appointee. However, this 'solution' raises the thorny question of the voting rights of the respective appointees, the determining of majorities, and appropriate appeal procedures — especially when the home-based state appointee is in the minority.[12]

On page 292 it is reported that 'we envisage a person holding a commission in one jurisdiction and a separate commission in another'. This would seem to imply that a federal-based dual appointee could be jointly appointed to only one state jurisdiction, almost as a quasi-resident (state) commissioner. The problem with this is that the organizational basis of the commission is inconsistent with what the Hancock Report apparently has in mind. The commission employs a panel system — which incidentally the Hancock Report endorses, at page 576, — where various personnel are allocated to particular industries or areas of work in order to develop specialist knowledge and skills. As is self-evident, industries operate across state boundaries. The states, on the other hand, are simply different lumps of geography whose formation was determined by the political dictates of the nineteenth century. It is quite conceivable that a federal-based dual appointee allocated to a particular state and with experience in industries *A*, *B*, and *C* may be confronted with problems in industries *X*, *Y*, and *Z*. Equally, if, as the Hancock Report implies, a federal-based dual appointee can be appointed to only one state, and such an appointee belongs to a particular federal panel, what state should that person be dually appointed to? As the report itself points out on page 577, 'moves towards the appointment of resident Commissioners would affect the allocation of work through panels formed on an industry basis'. A possible way around this problem could be to ensure that all federal dual appointees were commissioned in every state, though this in turn could prove to be an administrative nightmare. Alternatively the membership of panels could be increased from their current size of three or four to seven persons — one for each state and a senior tribunal member co-ordinating their work.[13]

Besides these administrative issues there may also be political problems associated with moving towards an integrated system. In particular, it is unlikely that the states would co-operate. An example is provided by the problems associated with *Moore* v *Doyle* (15 FLR 59), in which the federal and state branches of a union were recognized as separate legal entities; there is always the fear that this will encourage faction fighting.[14] Legislative changes recommended by the Sweeney Report (1974) to overcome the problems that arose in *Moore* v *Doyle* have not been enacted by state governments. The Hancock Report in fact acknowledges the failure of intergovernmental negotiations to bring about desired changes and, on the advice of legal counsel, recommends that the Commonwealth government should amend the Conciliation and Arbitration Act to enable members of a state union who so desire to be deemed members of the federal organ of the union[15] (see pp. 302–17). The question that needs to be answered is, if 'genuine negotiations' between state and federal governments cannot resolve the relatively minor problems of *Moore* v *Doyle*, why should they be more successful with the more fundamental issue of co-operative federalism and an integrated industrial relations system?

The Hancock Report makes a series of recommendations to restructure and reorganize the operation of federal tribunals to overcome the separation-of-powers doctrine established by the 1956 *Boilermakers* case (94 CLR 254). In that decision the High Court ruled that the same body that performed conciliation and arbitration functions could not also undertake the judicial functions of interpretation and enforcement. As a result, the old Arbitration Court was abolished and two new bodies — a commission and a court — were created. On pages 382 and 383 the Hancock Report lists a number of issues and problems associated with this separation of powers:

1 The inability of the commission to interpret or enforce awards has lessened its authority.
2 The system is complex and legalistic.
3 Arbitral and judicial powers should be rationalized.
4 Reforming the structure of the federal system will make the state and federal systems closer and enhance their integration.
5 Members of the court have a limited understanding of industrial relations realities.

The solution proposed by the Hancock Report to overcome these problems is to create two new federal institutions, namely an Australian Labour Court and an Australian Industrial Relations

Commission. Members of the court would hold dual appointments, being members of the commission also (according to legal advice received by the committee such dual appointments would survive High Court challenges). The chief judge of the court would also be president of the commission, and judges of the court would be appointed from among the ranks of legally qualified deputy presidential members of the commission. The report also recommended that a new position be created, that of vice-president of the commission, who would be a general aide to the president and who would supervise the work and functions of the commission.[16] The vice-president would sit on national wage cases, but would not be a member of the court. The evisaged structure of the federal tribunal would be as follows (it should be remembered that an unspecified number of personnel would also hold dual appointments in at least one state tribunal): commission president/chief judge of court; commission vice-president; legally qualified deputy president/judge of court; legally qualified deputy president; non-legally qualified deputy president; arbitration commissioner.

A number of criticisms can be made concerning both the analysis of the *Boilermakers* case and the Hancock Report recommendations. First, no evidence is provided to substantiate the various claims made concerning the so-called problems which flow from the *Boilermakers* case.

Second, the apparent need to enhance the authority of the federal arbitral body is inconsistent with statements made elsewhere in the report. On page 256, for example, the report observes that 'the federal conciliation and arbitration tribunal has become influential. Its influence has increased over the years as the nature of the Australian economy and Australian society have changed to reflect a more "national" approach.' Enhancement of its authority seems too to be at odds with the Hancock Report's rejection of the use of sanctions:

penalties can have no more than a limited role in the arbitration system; that they certainly cannot be its mainstay; and that attempts to impose a heavy burden upon them are likely to cause their collapse. Moreover, there is a danger that reliance on penalties to make the arbitration system work will discourage constructive thought about the changing nature of industrial relations and the need for adaption [*sic*] in the industrial relations system (p. 635).

If penalties are taboo, why enable members of the commission to be dually appointed and to preside in a labour court?

Third, while the present system *may* appear complex and legalistic — it is not certain that the parties experience difficulties; perhaps they cry foul only when they receive an unpalatable decision[17] — it is difficult to see how the Hancock Report's recommendations would in fact reduce any complexities or legalisms.

Fourth, it is not clear that revamping the federal tribunal would necessarily ensure its compatability with state tribunals. For a start, conciliation committees and industrial boards play a more important role in the states than they do at the federal level, and the federal system, as the Hancock Report points out on pages 30–7, is continually evolving. In addition, the respective state systems also undergo changes to their procedures and structures in response to the pressures placed on them by the parties that use them.

Fifth, the notion that the lack of industrial relations knowledge of members of the present court is an important source of its functional and performance problems (not specified in the report) is, as well as somewhat insulting to the personnel concerned, problematic. To the extent that there are 'problems', the nature of the cases and the possible protracted, tedious, and expensive legal battles may well be the cause. It is extremely difficult to see how a judge, even with the industrial relations wisdom of Solomon, would be able to reduce legalities and complexities when facing parties locked into extreme opposition. How can anyone be expected to placate both sides in particularly controversial and troublesome cases where a third party, in handing down a decision, establishes rights or privileges for one party that necessarily occur at the expense of an opponent? Furthermore, assuming adoption of the Hancock Report recommendations, it is conceivable that, in time, several members of the court/commission would specialize in court work (it would of course be argued that such specialization would be necessary to ensure proper and careful consideration of the important cases that come before the court for adjudication) and whatever the advantages derived from dual appointments, they would ultimately be lost.

Sixth, these recommendations may cause a series of personnel problems that could reduce the effectiveness of the federal tribunal(s). Besides the president/chief judge and vice-president, there are three types of deputy presidents plus arbitration commissioners. The danger here is that there are too many divisions among the 'officer corps' of the tribunal, which could produce rivalries and clashes. The court-based deputy presidential members may feel superior to other deputy presidents, upsetting the organizational base. It is not easy to see how the vice-president could succeed the president when he or she is not also a member of the court. Certain members of the court might regard themselves as being the appropriate presidential successor.

The Hancock Report endorses the oft-repeated claim that Australia has too many unions. On pages 457–8 the report maintains that the problems of too many unions include unnecessary competition, which leads to demarcation disputes; duplication and inefficient use of resources and the concomitant provision of limited services for members; and the difficulties employers experience in dealing with a large number of unions. Besides easing the amalgamation provisions of the Act (pp. 463–7), the major report recommendation on union reduction is abolition of unions with fewer than 1000 members, with qualifications for exceptional cases (pp. 461–2).

However, first, no research or information has been provided to establish whether unions with fewer than 1000 members are in fact involved in or associated with the so-called problem of Australia having too many unions. The committee could have profitably commissioned research on the role of small unions. Small unions are rarely involved in demarcation disputes (Wright, 1983, 1984); there is no evidence that they pose more of a problem for management than large unions; and if their members believed them to be so ineffectual, they could conceivably seek to join a large union either individually or collectively through amalgamation.

Table 4.1 Number of Unions with Fewer Than 1000 Members, by Jurisdiction, 1983

Jurisdiction	Number of Unions
Federal	31
New South Wales	34
Victoria	20
Queensland	11
South Australia	12
Western Australia	21
Tasmania	5
Australian Capital Territory	3
Northern Territory	3
Total	140

Source: Rawson and Wrightson (1985).
Note: In fifteen instances the membership details of a union were not given, and it has been assumed that the union had fewer than 1000 members.

Second, according to the Australian Bureau of Statistics, as at June 1986, 155 of Australia's 326 unions had fewer than 1000 members, but probably less than a fifth of these unions are federally registered and most small unions would therefore not be affected by the Hancock Report recommendations. Table 4.1, based on Rawson and Wrightson's (1985) registry of Australian unions, shows that only 31 (34 if those in the Australian Capital Territory are included) of the 140 unions with fewer than 1000 members are federally registered.[18] Indeed on page 22 the Hancock Report points out that 'Many small unions would be single state unions relying mainly on the decisions of local industrial tribunals.'

Third, implementation of this recommendation would probably have 'perverse' effects. There would almost certainly be a hostile, disruptive reaction from the small, normally passive (one never seems to hear anything from them) unions. It is also conceivable that federally deregistered small unions would seek registration at the state level — and if they have members in several states, there could be an increase in the number of small unions!

CONCLUSION

Most groups and organizations involved in industrial relations are subjective about reform: they class as reform those changes that they desire or favour. A conceptual and analytical definition defines reform as a change in procedural rules. Any and all changes in procedural rules constitute reform, irrespective of whether those involved in industrial relations desire change or approve of the changes. By this definition, groups and organizations may view any proposed reform very differently.

The committee of review charged with investigating and reporting on Australian industrial relations law and systems by early 1985 was active at a time when Australia was subject to the reign of wage indexation. In strongly endorsing the continuation of wage indexation the Hancock Report was seen as being anti-climactic and merely a celebration of the status quo, which begged the question of why the report was commissioned in the first place. The report is disappointing. It is poorly researched and poorly structured, lacks a theoretical base, is confused and contradictory, contains unfounded assertions, and makes no serious attempt to consider alternative proposals concerning the future development of Australian industrial relations. Three key recommendations of the report — the cross-commissioning of state and federal personnel; the creation of a new court and commission and the use of dual appointments; the abolition of unions with fewer than 1000 members — are unsound.

Fate, too, has not been kind to the Hancock Report. As the next chapter shows, vitually before the ink on the report was dry Australia's international and balance of payments problems combined to move Australia away from the wage indexation assumptions of the Accord, the summit, and the Hancock Report. In 1987 the Hawke government backed away from the report's recommended legislative changes, in the face of opposition from particularly employers.

NOTES

1 It should also be noted that two literature surveys were prepared for the Hancock Report (III, pp. 5–6).
2 The Hancock Report also commissioned the Roy Morgan Research

Centre to conduct a survey of national community attitudes to various aspects of industrial relations. See Hancock Report (III, pp. 207—45).

3 For an indication of the increasing number and variety of books recently published see the book-review and books-received sections of the *Journal of Industrial Relations*.

4 It should be remembered that this view was rejected in the Chapter 3 discussion.

5 New Zealand, the only other country that has a conciliation and arbitration system, was not included in the analysis.

6 See page 230 of the report for a similar statement.

7 The Hancock Report does not provide any evidence of Australian industrial relations problems — see pages 9—10 for example — manifesting in industrial disputes.

8 On page 7 the Hancock Report lists the objectives of government as reduction of levels of industrial disputation, protection of the rights of individuals, securing economic growth and progress, and wage equity.

9 While the Hancock Committee sponsored and financed the conference, it engaged both the Industrial Relations Research Centre and the National Institute of Labour Studies to perform the necessary organizational functions.

10 See, for example, Minister for Employment and Industrial Relations News Release, 20 May 1985, 121/85, Parliament House, Canberra, the *Australian*, 21 May 1985, and the *Australian Financial Review*, 24 May 1985.

11 In its decision in the *Ranger Uranium Mines* case, handed down on 16 December 1987, the High Court ruled that the commission had reinstatement powers.

12 Dual appointees from the state tribunals, and the state tribunals only, would do away with the need for a federal tribunal altogether.

13 The size of panels could be somewhat reduced where industries were not present in particular states.

14 In fact, research could have been commissioned to ascertain whether or not *Moore* v *Doyle*, or the law as such, is a crucial factor in union faction fighting.

15 It would be interesting to know whether these opinions were keyed to use of the 'corporations' or the 'external affairs' powers.

16 In some ways the functions of the vice-president are similar to those of the position of chief conciliation commissioner created by the 1947 amendments to the Conciliation and Arbitration Act.

17 For a discussion of the role of legalism see Cupper (1976).

18 Their data and the period they collected it in are different from the Australian Bureau of Statistics'.

CHAPTER 5

The Limits of Consensus

Chapter 3 examined the Hawke-led ALP government's early claim that consensus-based policies would achieve economic growth and recovery. From approximately the middle of 1985 consensus began to lose its glamour. The notion of consensus that was keyed to the Accord and the National Economic Summit Conference came under attack from three sources.

An unsuccessful attempt to introduce major taxation reform at the National Taxation Summit of July 1985 was the first indication of disaffection. Also, from 1985 and until 1987 Australia experienced major economic problems, particularly with respect to the international sector. Australia's balance of payments on current account were adverse, prices for Australian goods and the terms of trade declined, the exchange rate depreciated, and the international debt continually increased. In addition the Western world's stock-markets crashed in October 1987. These economic factors put great pressure on Australia's systems of wage determination and industrial relations regulation.

In addition, consensus and the corporatist policies of the Hawke government were trenchantly criticized by a group known as the New Right. They advocated a neo-classical market-based approach to overcome economic problems and preached a philosophy of management militancy to take on, if not abolish, unions and industrial tribunals.

This chapter focuses on the taxation summit and the various changes to Australian wage determination that flowed from international economic adversity and the stock-market crash. Chapter 6 will examine the ideas of the New Right.

THE NATIONAL TAXATION SUMMIT

The National Taxation Summit resulted from an undertaking given by Prime Minister Hawke during the December 1984 election campaign. Taxation had emerged as a political issue, owing to the increasing burden on pay-as-you-earn taxpayers; the inflation-induced bracket creep, whereby average-income earners were on the verge of paying marginal tax rates of 46 cents in the dollar; and problems associated with increasing tax avoidance and evasion, with 'bottom of the harbour' schemes being the most celebrated example. In calling the taxation summit the Hawke government hoped to achieve broad-based community support for major taxation reform.

In announcing the summit Hawke outlined nine principles which would guide the government in arriving at a taxation package.

First, there must be no increase in the overall tax burden, as measured by the share of Commonwealth Government tax revenue in gross domestic product through the Government's current term in office.

Second, any reform must continue the process already begun by the Government, and provide further cuts in personal income tax.

Third, taxation changes must contribute to smashing tax avoidance and evasion, which remain as features of the tax system which the Government inherited.

Fourth, any reform must lead to a simpler system, which therefore all Australians can understand more easily, and which therefore makes tax avoidance and evasion more difficult.

Fifth, any reform package must result in a tax system which is fairer, so that Australians are only required to pay tax according to their capacity to pay, and the overall system must be progressive.

Sixth, any tax reform must not disadvantage recipients of welfare benefits, and should reduce or remove 'poverty traps'.

Seventh, if any reform package which includes changes in indirect taxes is contemplated, it must be acceptable to the various groups in the Australian community whose response will determine whether we can maintain moderation in wage movements.

Eighth, any reform must provide the best possible climate for investment, growth and employment in Australia.

Ninth, any reform package must have widespread community support of a widely representative National Taxation Summit, of economic organisations and community groups (Draft White Paper, 1985, p. 2).

The draft white paper released before the summit outlined the dimensions of and the problems associated with tax collection at the Commonwealth level, as well as identifying a plan of action that the Hawke government wished to implement. The approach recommended by the draft white paper was to reduce the burden on pay-as-you-earn taxpayers by broadening the tax base; three options were listed. Option A comprised changing the tax rules or introducing new taxes concerning business and finance — fringe benefits, capital gains, negative gearing, primary-production losses, gold mining, petroleum and afforestation rebates, film industry concessions, write-off concessions to primary producers, concessional expenditure rebates, taxation of foreign-source income — and the introduction of a national identification system. It was estimated that the per annum revenue from option A was in the order of $1.8 billion. Option B involved the introduction of a broad-based consumption tax of 5 per cent which would provide an estimated revenue of $1.5 billion, or $3.3 billion when added to option A. Option C involved a broad-based consumption tax of 12.5 per cent which, it was estimated, after providing compensation for those on welfare and low incomes, would increase revenue by $6.8 billion, or $8.6 billion when combined with option A. The Hawke government went to the taxation summit batting for option C, because its revenue potential gave it greater scope to reduce pay-as-you-earn income tax.

The National Taxation Summit was held at Parliament House, Canberra, from 1 to 4 July 1985. Whereas 117 persons had attended the National Economic Summit Conference, in 1983, with the Australian Council of Social Services being the only Official Participant outside the triangle of governments, unions, and employers/business, the taxation summit listed 456 attendees (393, excluding observers, ministerial staff, and Commonwealth officials). Besides Commonwealth, state, and territory governments there were delegations from the Australian Democrats (the federal opposition declined an invitation to attend, an option they were not afforded at the economic summit), the Economic Planning Advisory Council (see Post-Summit Developments, Chapter 3), local government, the Australian Council of Trade Unions (ACTU), twenty-four employer/business/finance groups, eleven welfare/community groups, four women's organizations, five religious bodies, six professional associations, three tax bodies, the Australian Film Commission, the Australian Sports Commission, and a group of tax academics — a total of sixty-eight separate interest groups (eighty-four if observers, ministerial staff, and Commonwealth officials are included).

As with the economic summit, participants were asked to confine their speeches to between 10 and 15 minutes. Many delegations therefore circulated discussion papers. Excluding the chair's contribution, a total of 174 speeches were delivered over the four days, and 43 of these were given in a plenary session on the last day.

While congratulating Hawke on holding the summit, the great majority of speeches were simple exercises in self-interest. At the end of the first day, Commonwealth Treasurer Keating castigated speakers: 'I think the general tone of many of the comments has been divided, sectional and too uncompromising' (Taxation Summit, 1985, p. 54). Australian Democrats Senator Haines ruefully observed that 'most people's definition of tax reform has a tendency to mean reform which does not touch on their particular form of avoidance or evasion' (Taxation Summit, 1985, p. 106).

The various organizations represented at the taxation summit opposed the Hawke government's proposed reforms. All twenty-four of the employer/business/finance groups rejected option A (Taxation Summit, 1985, p. 160), claiming that such business/finance taxes would not provide the best possible climate for investment, growth, and employment. Furthermore, the ACTU and the welfare/community, religious, and women's groups rejected option C, because of the inflationary effects associated with a broad-based consumption tax and the anticipated harmful effects on low income earners and those dependent on welfare. Unlike the economic summit, the taxation summit did not produce a final communiqué. In what might be regarded as the quote of the taxation summit, Queensland Premier Sir Joh Bjelke-Petersen observed, 'I think the [Hawke] Government has probably achieved something. It has achieved a consensus — a consensus of opposition in the community' (Taxation Summit, 1985, p. 24).

Why was the Hawke government unable to achieve consensus

at the taxation summit[1] when it had been able to at the economic summit?

The negotiation of the Accord preceded the economic summit and dominated proceedings. There was no agreement between the Accord partners prior to the taxation summit. Moreover, Bill Kelty, the ACTU secretary, rejected the Hawke government's preferred option C on the first afternoon of the summit (1985, pp. 43−5). The employer/business/finance sector made sure that it did not appear as divided and ineffectual as it had at the economic summit and unanimously rejected option A. The Hawke government found itself isolated at the taxation summit.

The subject matter and issues of the two summits can be contrasted. The economic summit was an exercise in political rhetoric — about how co-operation and consensus would achieve economic growth and recovery. Hard decisions were either post-poned or delegated to other institutions such as the Australian Conciliation and Arbitration Commission, which was given the task of determining the future direction of wage determination. In addition, the final communiqué was vague, so as to minimize potential opposition. Finally, consensus is a 'motherhood' issue but tax is a specific issue. Interest groups invest time and energy and gather information about the costs or benefits of a tax system. Unlike economic growth and consensus, which pre-sumably everyone supports, taxation reform is not easily agreed on, because most groups and organizations wish to minimize their tax liabilities; if taxes have to be paid, let them be paid by someone else! At the taxation summit the Hawke government took on more than it could hope to achieve. Tax is not a con-sensus issue.

One reason for the economic summit's aura of success was that it was an apparently new approach by a new, ALP govern-ment with a new leader and a new political vocabulary. The economic summit was about process rather than substance. Stewart and Ballard observed that taxation summit participants 'were less easily moved by "the politics of the warm inner glow", and the consensus politics of Prime Minister Hawke' (Stewart and Ballard, 1985, p. 217).

The taxation summit was held when the Hawke government

had been in power for more than two years. Interest groups had arrived at an understanding of how to approach and pressure the Hawke government in seeking the realization of their organizational goals; they could build on the experience, and mistakes, of the economic summit; they were not overawed. As a result, the taxation summit was an exercise in substance rather than process, and the various interest groups sought to ensure that no extra taxes would be imposed on those whose interests they represented.

ECONOMIC CRISIS

In examining the British experience with corporatism Booth has commented that

corporatism in twentieth-century Britain appears to be little more than a technique of economic management operating within capitalism and developed during periods of national economic difficulty. When international slumps have overtaken the British economy, corporatist structures have been easily and painlessly dropped (Booth, 1982, p. 200).

With some qualifications a similar statement could be made about the Australian experience in the mid-1980s. From 1985 Australia was overtaken by a series of international economic problems that resulted in the abandonment of wage indexation and the introduction, in March 1987, of a two-tiered, more decentralized system of wage determination and industrial relations regulation by the Conciliation and Arbitration Commission. The stock-market crash of October 1987 placed further strains on Australian corporatism when the commission, in December 1987, decided to defer a national wage case increase because of the uncertainty this posed for Australia's international economic position. The main difference between the British experience observed by Booth and that of Australia in the 1980s has to do with difficulty and pain: whereas, according to Booth, British corporatist structures have been 'easily and painlessly dropped' when international slumps have overtaken the economy, in Australia the changes have taken more than two years to effect.

The Conciliation and Arbitration Commission reintroduced

wage indexation in 1983, claiming that it offered the best prospects for achieving economic growth and recovery. The commission hoped that national wage cases would be the major source of wage movements in Australia and in this respect the commission has been spectacularly successful. In its June 1986 national wage case decision the commission reported that between September 1983 and December 1985, 96 per cent of all award increases resulted from national wage case adjustments (NWC, 26 June 1986, p. 8).

The only significant increase outside wage indexation is that which occurred in the building industry. Following lengthy and protracted negotiations, unions and employers concluded an agreement which involved increases in allowances of $14.80 per week for labourers and $19.90 for craftspersons. The allowance included $7.50 for a building industry recovery procedure, which many saw as an exercise in cricumventing the commission's wage indexation principles. The commission refused to ratify this building industry recovery-procedure allowance. Building unions then sought to convert this allowance into a superannuation increase and successfully applied pressure on employers to establish a building industry superannuation scheme. The commission, for its part, maintained that superannuation should be considered under its wage indexation principles (Mulvey, 1984, 1985; Jenkins, 1986, pp. 114−22). Superannuation eventually became the basis of a national productivity claim mounted by the ACTU in the June 1986 national wage case. This experience with superannuation highlights the point made in Chapter 3 concerning problems and/or the weakness of a centralized system: an increase gained outside the system by a strategically placed group creates pressures for other groups to gain similar increases.

Table 5.1 summarizes the various wage-indexation decisions of the commission in the period 1983−86. The first two decisions were simple applications of the wage-indexation principles, where wages were increased in line with the previous two quarterly movements of the consumer price index (CPI). The 0.2 per cent fall in the CPI for the March and June quarters of 1984 resulted from the introduction of Medicare, the national health insurance scheme, which reduced the private health insurance component of the CPI. Following a conference with the commission's president the parties decided that there was no need for a hearing, reserving the right to make submissions concerning the 0.2 per cent at the next national wage case. In its April 1985 decision the commission discounted the 2.7 per cent increase in the September and December 1984 quarters by 0.1 per cent to 2.6 per cent, since that 'figure, derived by taking the CPI increase for the four quarters to December 1984, takes account of the CPI movement in the period for which there has been no review'. This was also consistent with the principle of maintaining real wages, a commission tenet and inherent in the Accord (NWC, 3 April 1985, p. 6).

In each of these decisions the commission reiterated that observance of and adherence to its wage indexation principles were essential if the Australia economy was to recover. The veracity of this view began to be seriously challenged in the second half of 1985. Notwithstanding the general economic recovery which had occurred in 1984 and 1985 (admittedly from a low base) — 5 per cent growth in 1984—85, recovery of profits, reductions in the level of unemployment to 8.1 per cent (from in excess of 10 per cent in 1983), and a reduction in the inflation rate, to 6.7 per cent — the economy was still confronting a number of significant problems. High real-interest rates and Australia's worsening balance of payments were a major source of alarm. Strong internal growth and a decline in the terms of trade combined to produce a balance of payments on current account deficit for 1984—85 in excess of $10 billion. In addition, Australia's international debt position had increased dramatically and the value of the Australian dollar had declined by nearly 20 per cent since December 1984.

The Hawke government initially indicated that it would seek to have the commission discount the forthcoming national wage case — the November 1985 decision, based on the previous six months' movement in the CPI (3.8 per cent) for the price effects of the devaluation of the Australian dollar (estimated by Treasury at 1.2 per cent) — to reduce inflationary pressures and Australia's worsening balance of payments problem. The ACTU objected to wage discounting, claiming that it would threaten the Accord. Eventually the ACTU and the Hawke government settled their agreement on wages, superannuation, and taxes that soon became known as the Accord Mark II. There were two parts to the Accord Mark II.

The first part was that the Hawke government would not argue for discounting in the case currently before the commission and the ACTU would defer its claim for a productivity increase, to which it was entitled by the principles that had been enunciated by the commission in its September 1983 decision, for six months. The commission subsequently endorsed this part of the Accord Mark II, in its November 1985 decision. While it noted that 'the need to adjust wage increases for the price effects of devaluation was not disputed by anyone', and stressed that it was not a 'rubber stamp', the commission found that the issue of discounting hinged on timing and that not to discount would 'have a negligible impact on the economy's competitive advantage brought about by the devaluation' (NWC, 4 November 1985, pp. 13–17).

The second part of the Accord Mark II was that in the 1986 national wage case, the ACTU and the Hawke government would agree to discount the six-monthly CPI adjustment for the price effects of the devaluation of the Australian dollar to a maximum of 2 per cent; wage and salary earners would be compensated for this loss by a reduction in the level of personal

Table 5.1   Alterations to Total Wage under Wage Indexation, 1983–86

Date		CPI Change (%)	Wage Change (%)
1983	March–June	4.3	4.3
	September–December	4.1	4.1
1984	March–June	−0.2	Nil
	September–December	2.7	2.6
1985	March–June	3.8	3.8
	September–December	4.3	2.3

Source: National wage case decisions.

income tax, to take effect from 1 September 1986; and the productivity case would be converted into a claim for extending and improving the superannuation entitlements of Australian workers, to be based on a 3 per cent wage equivalent which 'except in very isolated circumstances' was not to occur before 1 July 1986. The Hawke government also gave an undertaking to establish a national safety-net superannuation scheme to which employers would be required to contribute if they failed to provide cover for employees (Accord Mark II). Research by Peetz (1985) showed that at the end of 1984 approximately 45 per cent of Australian workers were covered by superannuation schemes. Part of the rationale for the superannuation deal was to reduce future budgetary problems associated with providing old-age pensions for Australia's ageing population.

The national employers vigorously opposed the ACTU's productivity/superannuation claim, maintaining that the commission did not have the constitutional authority to make determinations, as superannuation was not an industrial matter as implied by section 51, paragraph xxxv, of the Australian Constitution. On two occasions, 13 February and 27 March, the commission ruled that it had jurisdiction to make superannuation determinations. The employers subsequently sought relief in the High Court. On 15 May the High Court ruled in a unanimous decision that the commission had jurisdiction to hand down decisions with respect to the issue of superannuation (*Manufacturing Grocers* case, 15 May 1986).

During the hearing of the 1986 national wage case, there was a stream of bad news about the Australian economy. In the second half of 1985 the Hawke government had taken action to reduce demand pressures, in an attempt, among other things, to arrest Australia's balance of payments difficulties. While the level of unemployment continued to fall (to 7.6 per cent in June 1986), the economy nonetheless experienced negative growth in the December 1985 and March 1986 quarters. Despite the slowing down of the economy Australia's balance of payments problems continued. The prices received for Australian exports continued to decline, the balance of payments on current account deficit for 1985–86 was $13.8 billion, and the devaluation of the

Australian dollar continued; in the twelve months ending July 1986 the trade weighted index fell by 28 per cent.

Throughout the first half of 1986, discussions of the economy were characterized by gloom and doom as successive indicators of economic performance were published or as the Australian dollar hit record lows. To a large extent the fears crystallized when Commonwealth Treasurer Keating said on 14 May, on talk-back radio, that Australia was in danger of becoming a 'banana republic'.

On 11 June the prime minister delivered a nationally televised speech about the seriousness of the problems facing the economy and the need for belt-tightening and appropriate remedial action.[2] In a statement accompanying his speech Hawke supported the current applications before the commission, with the qualification that improvements to superannuation should be 'as limited as possible in 1986'. He also indicated that the 1 September tax cuts negotiated in the Accord Mark II might be deferred to 1 December, and that it might be necessary to argue for future wage discounting at the next national wage case. The prime minister's economic statement was formally submitted to the commission. The commission, in turn, invited written submissions from the respective participants in the national wage case, before handing down its decision.

The CPI increase for the September and December 1985 quarters, which the 1986 case was required to consider, was equal to 4.3 per cent. The commission accepted a figure of 1.91 per cent, as calculated by the Commonwealth Treasury, as the appropriate measure of the direct price effects of the devaluation of the Australian dollar. It also wished to take account of the indirect price effects, but pointed to the difficulties of finding an accurate measure. The commission decided to adopt a submission of the Commonwealth government, in that

taking into account the cost savings from the moderation, deferral and phasing in of the productivity claim, 2 per cent was an appropriate figure to offset completely the direct and indirect effect of devaluation on the CPI in 1985. It should be noted that under the ACTU/Commonwealth Agreement [the Accord Mark II], a 2 per cent reduction in income tax would take place in September 1986[3] to offset this adjustment (NWC, 26 June 1986, p. 15).

The wage increase based on changes in the CPI would be equal to 2.3 per cent. The commission also pointed out that 'the extraordinary length of the proceedings' associated with hearing the case[4] had 'provided employers with substantial cost relief which will go a long way to covering the indirect effects of devaluation' (NWC, 26 June 1986, p. 15).

Notwithstanding the fact that the Accord Mark II had inextricably linked the productivity—superannuation claim, the commission decided to examine the two issues separately. It first considered whether there was scope in the economy to grant a wage increase based on improvements in national productivity over the previous two and a half years. The commission directed attention to the original Accord and the April 1983 economic summit, which had created 'a legitimate expectation on the part of the unions and endorsed by employers and governments, that the real incomes of wage and salary earners should be increased in time in line with productivity'. The commission then said that because of the problems being experienced by the economy, particularly with respect to the international sector, 'no productivity-based claims ... will be considered during the term of the new package' (NWC, 26 June 1986, pp. 17–18). The new wage indexation principles announced by the commission did not include productivity as a ground for a national wage case increase.

The commission found that increases in national productivity which had occurred since 1983 had 'gone to restoring the health of the economy mainly by allowing a recovery in profits to take place and by slowing down the rate of inflation'. The commission then pointed out that because of the problems associated with Australia's international trading position, there was no scope for a productivity increase. The commission added that 'expectations however valid at the time they are generated, must be tempered by the rigours of the economic circumstances which prevail at the time they are to be met' and rejected 'the claim for a 4 per cent pay increase on account of productivity' (NWC, 26 June 1986, pp. 21, 22, 25).

The employers initially believed that they had achieved a major victory before the commission. On release of the decision they claimed that they had been successful in convincing the commission that economic circumstances did not justify a pro-ductivity-based increase.[5] Once they had had a chance to examine the decision more closely, their joy was short lived.

Unlike its statement on productivity the commission said of superannuation:

The expectations created by the ACTU/Commonwealth Agreement reinforced by the Government's guidelines have led to the establishment of new schemes by employers and unions and to active negotiations and understandings between them for contributions to new schemes and improved benefits to existing schemes ... If left outside the Commission's control, these developments, which are analogous to overaward pay-ments, could threaten the very foundation of the centralised system (NWC, 26 June 1986, p. 33).

The commission then said that it would be in the public interest for it to monitor and regulate any agreements reached by the parties with respect to superannuation. It was not prepared, however, to 'arbitrate to provide for superannuation as sought by the ACTU and the Commonwealth during the life of this package'.

Notwithstanding its refusal to countenance arbitration, the commission was nonetheless prepared to assist the parties in conciliation 'to ensure that agreements are implemented on an orderly and rational basis and are properly phased in, consistent with the state of the economy'. Furthermore, it would ratify superannuation agreements reached by the parties in the form of consent awards, as long as they were consistent with the following guidelines: they were to operate from a date deter-mined or approved by the commission in accordance with the commission's phasing-in procedure, but not before 1 January 1987[6] except in special and isolated circumstances approved by the commission; they were not to involve retrospective pay-ments of contributions; they were not to involve the equivalent of a wage increase in excess of 3 per cent of ordinary-time earnings of employees; they were to be consistent with the com-mission's principles and the determinations referred to in the decision; they were to be in accordance with the Common-wealth's Operational Standards for Occupational Superannuation Funds; the consent of the employers was to be genuine; and finally there is ambit.

The commission also foreshadowed that its new president, Mr Justice Maddern, would call a conference of the parties to a special national wage case to 'examine the guidelines and procedures to be adopted in the consideration of claims relating to superannuation'. The commission also said that endorsed superannuation agreements would 'not result in discounting of national wage case decisions[7]'; nor would they be treated as a breach of the unions' 'no extra claims' undertaking as required by the wage indexation principles. It added, however, that it would 'obviously have regard to any industrial action imposed on an employer in determining whether or not there is genuine agreement' (NWC, 26 June 1986, p. 34).

It is difficult to follow the logic of the commission's handling of the productivity–superannuation claim; it is ambiguous, confused, and contradictory. There are essentially three problems with the decision. First, while the commission apparently rejected the claim for a productivity increase because of the 'persistent and serious balance of payments problem' confronting the economy, it nonetheless gave its imprimatur to the superannuation claim, which had been based on improvements in productivity. It is difficult to understand how the commission, in rejecting a productivity increase, could at the same time enable superannuation claims based on improvements in productivity to proceed.

Second, as the commission refused to arbitrate the superannuation claim during the life of its new indexation package it foreshadowed a superannuation national wage case and developed a set of guidelines to aid the parties in negotiating superannuation deals.

Third, the commission appears, in saying that superannuation disputes would not be linked to the no-extra-claims clause and that endorsed superannuation deals would not be subjected to wage discounting at future national wage cases, to have invited unions to make use of industrial action in pursuing superannuation deals with employers. As the industrial parties know, 'genuine agreements' emerge on termination of disputes.

Some confusion resulted from the no-extra-claims aspect of the commission's superannuation decision. The ACTU interpreted this to mean that its stronger affiliates were able to push ahead with superannuation claims in the field in an attempt to secure early commitment or agreement from employers, that affiliated unions would only need to give a qualified commitment to the commission's principles, and that industrial action could be used in pursuing superannuation claims. The national employers worried about how superannuation could be phased in without jeopardizing the economy, and feared that a dual system would be created, where stronger unions would not commit themselves to the centralized system, while weaker unions would. They called on the ACTU to ensure that its affiliates would show collective commitment to centralization and hinted that if such a commitment was not forthcoming, they would urge the commission to abandon its decision.

Why the commission refused to arbitrate the superannuation claim, especially since the High Court had in May confirmed its power to do so, provokes speculation. The commission, if it had so desired, could have simply refused the claim, emphasizing Australia's balance of payments problems. Alternatively it could have decided to grant the claim, combining it with the guidelines that accompanied its 'non-arbitrated' decision. Given the commission's preparedness to enunciate superannuation guidelines, it is somewhat surprising that it decided not to arbitrate.

One possible explanation could be the institutional needs of the commission. The commission, like any institution in society, seeks to enhance its role and stature and to protect itself from criticism and attack. As the Chapter 1 discussion of theories of regulation revealed, the commission is involved in the difficult task of devising solutions to the various and numerous problems associated with industrial relations regulation and of having to negotiate and deal with strong and resourceful organizations that have different goals and objectives (Dabscheck, 1980, 1983, 1986; Romeyn, 1980). In addition, this case occurred at a time of economic strain, highlighted by Australia's balance of payments problems. The commission may have been fearful of the consequences of acceding to the superannuation claim via arbitration, but was perhaps not prepared to stop the superannuation push because of the expectations created by the Accord Mark

II. By refusing to arbitrate, and forcing superannuation onto the field, the commission may have embarked on a strategy designed to protect itself from future criticism should the economy worsen.

A second, less sophisticated explanation may be that the commission decided not to arbitrate because the members of the Full Bench could not agree among themselves on whether the claim should be granted. Though a decision inheres unanimity, the confused and contradictory nature of the decision on super-annuation suggests a split among the members of the Full Bench. Perhaps the Full Bench was fearful of the criticisms likely to be directed at the commission if majority and minority decisions were handed down, especially as this was an important case. An informal agreement to sink and/or conceal their differences[8] will be shown below to be the most likely explanation.

Because of the confusion surrounding the commission's decision on the use of industrial action by unions pursuing superannuation Mr Justice Maddern held a series of conferences with the parties on 7 and 8 July, and issued a statement 'in order to avoid future misunderstanding'. His six-page statement basically restates the commission's position as expressed in its decision. With respect to the no-extra-claims clause and superannuation, it states:

The terms of the undertaking do not necessarily prohibit industrial action. Indeed it would be unrealistic of us to expect an undertaking by the unions that they will not engage in any industrial action particularly in the light of our decision not to arbitrate on superannuation. However, we emphasise the view expressed in the decision that industrial action is unnecessary and this statement cannot be interpreted as condoning indus-trial action. We have said we will consider industrial action in detail in determining whether a breach of undertaking occurs. In particular, we indicated in the National Wage Case decision that the superannuation Full Bench will have regard to industrial action in determining whether or not there is a genuine superannuation agreement (Maddern, 1986, pp. 4−5).

The statement did not, however, end the confusion. A number of unions, in seeking to gain the 2.3 per cent increase, gave only qualified commitment to the commission's wage indexation prin-ciples, consistent with ACTU policy, and reserved the right to use industrial action in pursuit of superannuation. Some members of the commission were prepared to accept this qualified commitment. Mr Justice Alley, however, on 21 July refused to accept the qualified commitment provided by unions in the building industry. He maintained that such commitments were inconsistent with the commission's recently determined wage indexation principles.[9]

Two days later Mr Justice Williams, the second most senior member of the commission, who had also been a member of the Full Bench in the 1986 national wage case, deferred the 2.3 per cent increase for workers in the metal trades, because of the need to confer with Mr Justice Maddern as to the meaning of his 8 July statement. In noting Mr Justice Alley's earlier decision, Mr Justice Williams is reported to have said, 'It is vital that there be consistency and cohesion in the manner of dealing with this issue by the Commission'.[10]

After conferring with Mr Justice Maddern, and after the metal unions had changed the form of their commitment, Mr Justice Williams subsequently granted the 2.3 per cent increase. The metal unions altered their qualified commitment to include the statement 'it is understood that the right to take industrial action is not prohibited'. Mr Justice Williams is reported to have said that the metal unions' altered form of (qualified) commitment 'is in effect a statement of a general trade union principle. It has to be seen in this context and does not alter in substance the specific commitment given to the wage fixation principles.'[11]

Notwithstanding its discounting of the CPI for the price effects associated with the devaluation of the Australian dollar the commission decided to introduce a new set of wage indexation principles which, with the obvious exception of the inclusion of superannuation guidelines and the removal of changes in national productivity as a ground for future national wage case increases, were similar to those it had determined in September 1983. However, the condition of the economy, particularly with respect to the international sector, and the associated need for discounting enshrined in the June 1986 decision, was logically inconsistent with maintaining wage indexation. It seemed it would only be a matter of time before an alternative system would be put into place.

TRYING TWO TIERS

At the next national wage case all of the major parties agreed that, given the current and anticipated economic problems, wage indexation was no longer sustainable. The commission formally brought wage indexation to an end on 23 December 1986 (NWC, 23 December 1986). While there was broad agreement among the parties to develop a two-tiered system, there were differences over how it should operate. The commission decided to defer making a decision until the parties had had a chance to confer. After a number of conferences, on 10 March 1987 the commission announced its decision on the operation of a two-tiered system.

The two-tiered system is a mix of centralization and decentralization. The first tier comprises traditional national wage cases and it operates in two parts. In its 10 March 1987 decision the commission awarded a $10 per week increase as a first part of the system. The second part comprised a hearing, to start in October 1987, to consider a further increase which 'shall not exceed the equivalent of a 1.5 per cent increase in wages and salaries' (NWC, 10 March 1987, p. 35). The second tier comprises decentralized, industry-by-industry, or award-by-award, cases. The grounds for second-tier increases are restructuring and changes to improve efficiency, including work-value streamlining and removal of anomalies and inequities. Second-tier increases, and the new restructuring and efficiency principle in particular, are designed to encourage decentralized decision making and to enhance the attainment of micro-economic efficiency. The commission has placed a 4 per cent limit on second-tier increases. Subject to ratification by the commission the parties can reach agreements on second-tier increases. If they are unable to agree, the commission will arbitrate and award up to 2 per cent from not before 1 September 1987, with a further 2 per cent from not before 1 July 1988.

In addition the commission announced new procedures to govern the handling of superannuation applications. As it had in its (in)decision of June 1986, the commission placed a 3 per cent limit on superannuation increases. Again, subject to ratification by the commission the parties could agree to such an increase. If the parties are unable to agree, the commission will arbitrate and award up to 1.5 per cent not before 1 January 1988, with the second 1.5 per cent to operate from not before 1 January 1989. The commission announced that it would review the package in May 1988.

By the end of 1987 approximately 25 per cent of the workforce had gained second-tier increases, but the phasing in was not free of problems. First, restructuring and efficiency (or productivity) changes may be one-off exercises, incapable of sustaining a decentralized system of wage determination. Second, the restructuring and efficiency principle discriminates against unions that are weakly organized at the grass-roots level — for example in the white collar, service, and predominantly female sectors — and favours those unions and their membership where it is relatively easy to measure productivity and/or in which there are a number of well-entrenched restrictive work practices. Third, the second tier may have a perverse effect. If in the future the principal way to obtain a wage increase is by restructuring and becoming more efficient, this may encourage unions and their members to jealously hold on to and/or develop new restrictive work practices.

The October 1987 stock-market crash came just as the commission was set to consider the second part of the first-tier national wage case increase. The ACTU converted the 1.5 per cent increase 'available' to a flat amount of $7 per week; the Hawke government argued for a $6.50 increase; the national employers maintained that the case should be adjourned until the May 1988 review of the commission's principles. In its decision the commission said that 'Movements in share prices alone have nothing to do with the outcome of national wage cases and we would not alter the decision we would otherwise make in this case simply because of the decline in share market prices.' The commission was particularly concerned, however, with Australia's international economic performance: 'it is of critical importance that no step be taken now that may handicap Australia's ability to cope with the rapid adjustments in the world economy now taking place. Additional time is needed to allow an assessment to be made of possible adverse effects on the economy' (NWC, 17 December 1987, p. 13). The commission deferred its decision and stated that it would reconvene on 28 January 1988.

The commission, by handing down its decision just before the Christmas—January holiday period, ensured that there would be no industrial action by unions frustrated with the decision. The ACTU secretary, Bill Kelty, was nevertheless critical of the commission, and several prominent union leaders threatened industrial action in early 1988 unless the commisssion revised its decision.

On 28 January 1988 the commission reconvened. After reviewing the additional evidence and the submissions the commission handed down its decision on 5 February 1988. The commission found that in the period since the stock-market crash 'there has not occurred such a change in relevant indicators as would reflect serious and adverse consequences of the collapse in share prices'. It also concluded that 'the serious consequences predicted by some observers in October have not eventuated ... the ill effects have not been drastic or immediate'. The commission also stated that

it appears that the economic uncertainty which is now apparent will remain for an indefinite period. To further adjourn these proceedings because of 'uncertainty' would appear to make an open-ended commitment which would be inconsistent with any rational wage policy. We believe that it would be counter-productive and we are not prepared to delay an increase (NWC, 5 February 1988, p. 5).

The commission decided to grant an increase of $6 per week. The net effect of the October 1987 stock-market crash was to delay the second part of the first-tier national wage case by seven weeks.

CONCLUSION

The July 1985 National Taxation Summit and the international economic decline that had set in in the mid-1980s exposed the limits of consensus-based policies and raised doubts about the applicability or usefulness of corporatist theory to Australia.

While Australian industrial relations in the 1980s may appear corporatist, the taxation summit showed that in other political—economic areas Australia was set to follow a (societal) pluralist model, with (see Chapter 1) interest groups pursuing self-interest rather than the common good as defined for them by the Hawke government.

International economic problems have brought changes to Australian wage determination and the system of industrial relations regulation. In September 1985 the ACTU and the Hawke Labor government negotiated the Accord Mark II, which recognized that wage indexation was no longer economically sustainable, given a depreciating Australian dollar (the implementation of the decision was delayed until the middle of 1986). As international economic problems continued, the Accord partners and the national employers agreed to formally terminate wage indexation and institute a two-tiered system of industrial relations regulation. The two-tiered system is designed to encourage restructuring and efficiency changes at the microeconomic level, while recognizing a lesser role for national wage cases. Following the October 1987 stock-market crash the commission delayed making a decision in a national wage case, until February 1988, because of uncertainty surrounding Australia's position in the world economy.

Three points should be made concerning these changes. The first — an issue that has been canvassed in Chapter 2 — concerns the flexibility or adaptability of Australian industrial relations. From September 1983 to September 1985 Australia was governed by wage indexation. The Accord Mark II, while continuing with a centralized system, saw a switch from wage indexation to a system more sensitive to Australia's international economic plight. At the end of 1986 and in early 1987 Australia switched again, from a centralized system to one that combined centralization and decentralization. While it is unclear what impact the stock-market crash will ultimately have, Australia will almost certainly develop and experiment with yet another system of industrial relations regulation in the near future.

Second, while national employers were not involved in drawing up the Accord Mark II (or the Accord Mark I, for that matter), they participated in development of the two-tiered system. To the national employers the attractions of the two-tiered system were that it marked the end of what they regarded as a slavish dependence on wage indexation, enhanced the importance of productivity as a factor in wage determination, and facilitated a move to a more decentralized system of industrial relations regulation. The two-tiered system is the second time in the 1980s that the national employers have been satisfied by, or at least not publicly opposed to, a wage determination system operated by the commission (the other occasion was the wages freeze). The national employers have in the 1980s committed themselves only to wage determination systems that have eschewed wage indexation. In other words, if the national employers had been involved with the Accord partners, and agreements had been reached that were satisfactory to the employers, Australia would not have had wage indexation in the 1980s.

Third, it is unclear whether the two-tiered system should be regarded as an exercise in corporatism. The two-tiered system combines elements of centralization and decentralization. Is corporatism a sufficiently flexible concept to incorporate decentralized decision making? Assuming an affirmative response, it would seem that what is notable about the Australian case is the flexibility or adaptability of its corporatism. In this chapter we have examined three variants: first, a system based on wage indexation; second, a system that discounted wage indexation for the price effects associated with the devaluation of the Australian dollar; third, the two-tiered system.

NOTES

1 Groenewegen (1985) claims that, from the perspective of problems traditionally associated with the politics of tax reform, the taxation summit was a moderate success.
2 For the full text of the prime minister's speech, and his accompanying economic statement, see the *Australian Financial Review*, 12 June 1986.
3 Hawke's 11 June speech indicated that the tax cuts could be deferred for up to three months.

4 The case started in early February, with the decision not being handed down until 26 June. Fifty sitting days were involved.

5 See the *Sydney Morning Herald*, the *Australian Financial Review*, and the *Australian*, 27 June 1986.

6 This had been requested in Hawke's 11 June speech.

7 This needs to be contrasted with a statement on the same page: 'the number and order of agreements will be carefully monitored to ensure that it will not be necessary to discount in National Wage Cases'.

8 There is a precedent for this. In the 1953 *Basic Wage Inquiry* the members of the Court reached an informal agreement to conceal their differences in an apparently unanimous decision (Dabscheck, 1983, pp. 143–7).

9 See the *Sydney Morning Herald* and the *Australian*, 22 July 1986.

10 See the *Sydney Morning Herald*, the *Australian Financial Review*, and the *Australian*, 24 July 1986.

11 See the *Sydney Morning Herald* and the *Australian*, 26 July 1986.

CHAPTER 6

New Right or Old Wrong?

Early in 1986 the inaugural meeting of the H. R. Nicholls Society was held in Melbourne. A series of papers were delivered, the proceedings of which were published as *Arbitration in Contempt*. What distinguishes the H. R. Nicholls Society from other groups interested in industrial relations is their commitment to management militancy and confrontation, and aggressive advocacy of the principles of neo-classical laissez-faire market capitalism. The H. R. Nicholls Society is committed to labour-market deregulation and therefore reduction of the power of, if not elimination of, trade unions and industrial tribunals. The labour market is seen as the source of Australia's economic problems. According to the H. R. Nicholls Society it is only by deregulating the labour market and allowing business to make hard-headed economic decisions, free of the interference of governments, industrial tribunals, and trade unions, that the problems of the economy will ever be resolved.

Various members of the H. R. Nicholls Society, and like-minded persons, have been developing and espousing their views in a variety of publications. *Quadrant* and the *IPA Review* regularly include articles criticizing labour-market regulation, industrial tribunals, and trade unions. Other writings in this genre include those by Stone (1984a), West (1984), Hyde and Nurick's edited volume (1985), McGuinness (1985), and Leard (1986).

The H. R. Nicholls Society gained national attention during a dispute at the Robe River project, in Western Australia's Pilbara region, in August and September 1986. The company involved, Peko-Wallsend, adopted a confrontationist stance in locking out over 1000 workers in an unilateral attempt to change some 284 work practices to enhance efficiency and profitability. Work resumed after an order by the Western Australian Industrial Appeals Court that the issues in dispute should be resolved under the auspices of the Western Australian Industrial Relations Commission.

The commission found that Peko-Wallsend had unfairly sacked its workforce and ordered it to pay each worker three weeks' back-pay without any loss of entitlement or continuity of employment. It also ruled that it would not interfere with the company's right to manage its own affairs, unless the union could prove that there was a need for the involvement of the commission. Peko-Wallsend was again in the news in October 1986, when Besco Batteries, a subsidiary in Sydney, closed down its operations, giving its 500-strong workforce half an hour's notice.

As the Robe River dispute unfolded it was revealed that Peko-Wallsend's chief executive, Charles Copeman, was chairman of the H. R. Nicholls Society. In late August and early September 1986 the media discovered the H. R. Nicholls Society; its goals and members received widespread coverage.[1] As more information concerning the society became available it was revealed that its members had been involved in recent confrontations and victories over unions in the South East Queensland Electricity Board, Mudginberri, and Dollar Sweets disputes. It also appeared that the ideas of the H. R. Nicholls Society had received support, if not endorsement, from certain sections of the federal Liberal Party. Williams (1986b) has reported that members of the society have been involved in developing the party's industrial relations policy and draft legislation in readiness for a return of the Liberals.

The goals, ideology, and tactics of the H. R. Nicholls Society have been criticized by a number of groups and organizations, not only unions. Prime Minister Hawke described the society as 'political troglodytes and lunatics' whose confrontationist style could only lead to industrial relations chaos.[2] Both Steele Hall and Ian Macphee, prominent federal Liberal members of Parliament, have also voiced criticisms. Hall is concerned that adoption of the policies of the H. R. Nicholls Society will link the Liberals with right wing extremists.[3] Macphee is critical of the 'politics of despair' being generated and the rejection of 'the notion of compassion that is crucial to any enlightened liberal society'.[4]

Brian Powell, chief executive of the Australian Chamber of Manufactures, described the New Right as 'classic fascists', deploring their use of confrontationist tactics. He maintained that the need is

to face our problems with unity and that destructive elements should not distract us from working together to improve our living standards ... If Australia is to overcome the present difficulties it will be by pulling together, not by pulling apart (*Sydney Morning Herald*, 3 October 1986).[5]

The Confederation of Australian Industry (CAI) has trenchantly criticized the H. R. Nicholls Society over its view that Australia's economic and industrial relations problems would be resolved by abolishing industrial tribunals, saying that these are 'escapist fantasies' (CAI, 1986).

In terms of its potential for divisiveness, both in the industrial relations arena and in broader political terms, the closest precursor to the H. R. Nicholls Society would be the Movement, or Industrial Groups, led by B. A. Santamaria during the 1940s and 1950s. The Movement, among other things, was involved in a campaign to 'clean up' trade unions and the Australian Labor Party (ALP), to rid both of communist or socialist ideas and personnel. The tensions that developed from struggles between 'communists', the Movement, and traditional ALP members and union officials resulted in an emotional and traumatic split of the ALP in 1955 (Murray, 1970; Ormonde, 1972).

Members of the H. R. Nicholls Society, and like-minded persons, are not critical of unions because of their adherence to communist or socialist ideology.[6] Rather, their criticism is that the system has allowed the unions to gain too strong a foothold; it is the triumvirate of big government, big unions, and big business that is the cause of Australia's economic problems. The co-operative, almost capitalistic ethos of unions, and the fact that they are seen to have an input into national economic decision making, is resented by the H. R. Nicholls Society. The Movement never sought the abolition of unions; it sought their capture (see Chapter 2), to ensure that they were directed and that they behaved in a manner consistent with the Movement's ideology. The H. R. Nicholls Society, on the other hand, sees no real role for unions and industrial tribunals.

This chapter discusses why H. R. Nicholls was chosen as the society's 'mascot', and the factors that contributed to formation of the society. The notion of the Industrial Relations Club, the role of industrial tribunals, the use of equity courts and common law contracts, and the role of markets, with particular reference to the issue of youth unemployment, are examined.

H. R. NICHOLLS AND THE H. R. NICHOLLS SOCIETY

At the end of 1984, Rickard published a biography of Henry Bournes Higgins, the second president of the Commonwealth Court of Conciliation and Arbitration, from 1907 to 1921 (Rickard, 1984). Rickard indicates that Higgins's role was important in the establishment and development of industrial tribunals to regulate disputes between unions and employers. In 'A New Province for Law and Order', in the *Harvard Law Review* Higgins maintained that

the process of conciliation, with arbitration in the background, is substituted for the rude and barbarous process of strike and lockout. Reason is to displace force; the might of the State is to enforce peace between industrial combatants as well as between other combatants; and all in the interests of the public (Higgins, 1915, p. 14).

Higgins's 'new province for law and order' in industrial relations was part of a wider intellectual/political movement that gained prominence in Australia at the turn of the century. Liberalism, or progressivism, as it has been alternatively labelled (Roe, 1984), rejects the principles of laissez-faire capitalism and slavish dependence on the forces of supply and demand. Liberals/ progressives advocate that the state should introduce reforms to counterbalance the undesirable consequences of concentrations of wealth and power. A technique of 'government' much favoured by liberals/progressives is the creation of regulatory agencies, staffed by independent and disinterested experts, who regulate and supervise the behaviour of economic agents (see Chapter 1 for a discussion of theories of regulation).

Rickard (1984, pp. 186–7) provides details of a contempt of court case involving Higgins and H. R. Nicholls, the editor of the Hobart *Mercury* from 1883 to 1912. The background to the case was a clash between Higgins and Attorney H. E. Starke (who was subsequently appointed to the High Court) over the latter's alleged disrespect to the Fisher Labor government, or what Higgins referred to during the clash as 'those above us'. On 7 April 1911 Nicholls published an editorial, 'A Modest Judge', which began as follows:

> Mr Justice Higgins is, we believe, what is called a political Judge, that is, he was appointed because he had well served a political party. He, moreover, seems to know his position, and does not mean to allow any reflections on those to whom he may be said to be indebted for his judgeship (Hobart *Mercury*, 7 April 1911).

Higgins had in fact been appointed to the High Court in 1906, and subsequently the Arbitration Court in 1907, by Liberal Prime Minister Alfred Deakin. Higgins took umbrage at the editorial and persuaded Attorney-General William Morris Hughes to initiate contempt of court proceedings. Nicholls's attorney admitted that the offending sentences 'were inaccurate' in that Higgins had not been appointed by a Labor government and 'expressed ... regret for their publication' (12 CLR 280, p. 283). The withdrawal and apology by Nicholls, however, does not figure prominently in the High Court decision. Chief Justice Griffith, speaking on behalf of the High Court, found that while 'a publication concerning a Judge may be libellous, it is not a contempt ... unless it is calculated to obstruct or interfere with the course of justice or the administration of the law'. He added, in a passage which suggests that there may have been a degree of tension between Higgins and some of his brother judges, that

> if any Judge of this Court or of any other Court were to make a public utterance of such character as to be likely to impair the confidence of the public, or of suitors or any class of suitors in the impartiality of the Court in any matter likely to be brought before it, any public comment on such an utterance, if it were a fair comment, would, so far from being a contempt of Court, be for the public benefit, and would be entitled to similar protection to that which comment upon matters of public interest is entitled under the law of libel (12 CLR 280, p. 286).

Shaw and Harris, in examining this case, have claimed that 'it represents a pretty hollow forensic victory' for H. R. Nicholls. They also believe that it does not represent any heroic episode in Australian industrial relations or law. An erroneous and intemperate editorial, which its author was not prepared to defend, was held not in any technical contempt of the High Court (Shaw and Harris, 1986, p. 12).

To the labour-market deregulators of the mid-1980s, however, this case is regarded as a significant victory: Nicholls successfully took on and challenged the authority of Higgins and the Arbitration Court. The society's scorn, derision, and contempt for Higgins are boundless; Evans, a member of the steering committee that formed the society, has described Higgins as 'one of Australia's most damaging and delusioned nut cases' and as a 'lawyer gone quite crazy' (Hyde and Nurick, 1985, pp. 32, 38).[7] Higgins is seen as being responsible for not only the creation of industrial tribunals but also — despite the intervening eighty years — the current problems for the Australian economy.

The society's choice of H. R. Nicholls as mascot is curious. Nicholls's only excursion into industrial relations, if it can be called that, was his editorial criticizing Higgins. An obituary in the *Tasmanian Mail* pointed out that Nicholls was an early advocate of the view that mining companies should be held responsible for accidents which resulted from neglect or proper precautions. He had in fact been at the Eureka Stockade, in 1854, but withdrew before the attack took place, because 'he realised that defence was hopeless, and did not approve of the methods adopted for remedying what he recognised to be hardship and injustice suffered by the miners' (*Arbitration*, p. 329). While H. R. Nicholls was undoubtedly fearless in expressing his ideas, he does not seem to have possessed the necessary credentials for leading a frontal attack on perceived excesses of government regulation and controls.

If the labour-market deregulators of the mid-1980s were looking for a hero, they might have chosen one of Australia's early entrepreneurs — someone of the ilk of BHP's G. D. Delpart, or Essington Lewis. If they were looking for opponents of Higgins in the industrial relations arena, H. V. McKay or W. G. Barger, who successfully challenged the constitutionality (6 CLR 41) of Higgins's famous decision in the 1907 *Harvester* case (2 CAR 1), which established a minimum wage of seven shillings (70 cents) a day for an adult unskilled male labourer,[8] are more credible contenders. Or if they were looking for Higgins's nemesis why not choose William Morris Hughes (Lee, 1980)?

In an H. R. Nicholls Society letter to potential members, reference is made to 'a crucial debate' concerning the reform of Australian industrial relations. The letter states that 'there needs to be an increase both in the tempo of the debate and of its depth and breadth of intellectual content' (*Arbitration*, p. 14). The letter also makes particular reference to an announcement by the Hawke Labor government to implement recommendations of the Hancock Report (see Chapter 4). The report, among other things, expressed strong support for and offered recommendations to enhance a system of centralized wage determination based on wage indexation.

The formation of the H. R. Nicholls Society[9] can probably be most usefully explained as a reaction to the Accord (Mark I and Mark II). First, while the Accord was hailed as being responsible for the growth which occurred in 1983 and 1984, it was seen as being responsible for the downturn and associated balance of payments problems that occurred in 1985 and 1986.

Second, the Hawke Labor government's approach to employers has had the effect of destabilizing national employer associations, particularly the CAI, and has encouraged the formation of rival employer groups and splinter groups. The employers were not included in the architecting of the Accord, either Mark I or Mark II. Hawke has tended to play rival employer groups off against each other and/or to deal with them on a one-to-one basis.[10] While the relationship between the Hawke government and the ACTU may appear corporatist, its relationship with employers/capital is more consistent with pluralism.[11] Since the election of the Hawke Labor government two rival national employer groups have formed: the Business Council of Australia (BCA), in 1983, and the Australian Federation of Employers, in 1986.

Third, the Australian Conciliation and Arbitration Commission's decisions in national wage cases, in the period September 1983 to June 1986, followed the Accord. As a result, national employer representatives were not able to point to any major victories they had achieved before the commission. This opened them to charges of 'gutlessness' and 'spinelessness' and fostered the notion that alternative and more militant organizations were needed to represent the views and interests of Australian employers.

While the H. R. Nicholls Society criticizes and bemoans the extent of the state's intervention in industrial relations, it simultaneously calls for increased powers for the state and/or the need for a strong government to stand up to and take on trade unions. In addition, it wishes to abolish industrial tribunals and regulate industrial relations through equity courts and common law contracts. The objection to industrial tribunals is that they resolve disputes through conciliation and arbitration and lack enforcement powers against unions that transgress awards or make use of the strike weapon, whereas the equity courts can enforce common law contracts and award damages for breaches of contract (*Arbitration*, Chapter 6). Given the H. R. Nicholls Society's advocacy of the need for increased reliance on the government and courts to enforce agreements it is somewhat difficult to comprehend how the adoption of its policies would see an end to or diminution of state intervention. It would be more correct to describe the society as wishing to strengthen those parts of the state (government, equity courts, and police) that it regards as being (potentially) favourable to its interests, and weakening other sections (industrial tribunals) that it sees as being inimical to its interests.

The H. R. Nicholls Society is confronted by a major constitutional problem in seeking to strengthen the role and industrial relations powers of the Commonwealth government. Under the Constitution the Commonwealth government is severely limited in its ability to become involved in industrial relations. The Commonwealth government's major industrial relations power resides in section 51, paragraph xxxv, of the Constitution, which empowers it to make laws with respect to 'conciliation and arbitration for the prevention and settlement of industrial disputes extending beyond the limits of any one state'. The Constitution forces the Commonwealth government to delegate industrial relations powers to industrial tribunals, tribunals that have jealously guarded their independence and asserted that they are not hamstrung by the government of the day. While state governments are not encumbered by the same constitutional constraints as the Commonwealth government, and enjoy direct industrial relations powers, all have established tribunals to regulate industrial relations within their particular jurisdictions.

If the H. R. Nicholls Society were successful in abolishing federal tribunals, unions and employers could seek award coverage from the relevant state tribunal. The society is hopeful of finding some means to prevent this; it wishes to sidestep the federal basis of Australian industrial relations.

There are three avenues available for locating industrial relations powers with the Commonwealth government, away from both state governments and federal tribunals. First, the Commonwealth could seek the co-operation of the states and ask them to cede powers to the Commonwealth government. It is unlikely that state governments would agree to such a request. They would wish to maintain state rights and would not wish to forgo the power and patronage traditionally associated with their industrial relations powers.

Second, the Commonwealth government could seek to change the Constitution via a referendum. The major problem with this is that seven previous attempts to enhance the Commonwealth government's industrial relations powers — in 1911, 1913, 1919, 1926, 1944, 1946, and 1973 (the 1973 referendum was concerned with power over wages) — have proved to be unsuccessful.

Third, the High Court could reinterpret the Constitution and make use of other powers — trade and commerce, corporations, and external affairs — to grant the Commonwealth government direct industrial relations powers. Spry has suggested that it would be possible for the Commonwealth government to assume direct industrial relations powers, through carefully drafted legislation, which would not only enable the abolition of federal industrial tribunals but, more significantly, 'would prevent the states from continuing with or enlarging the regulation of industrial relations' (*Arbitration*, p. 125). This view has been challenged by other constitutional lawyers (Williams, 1986b).

The H. R. Nicholls Society wants an industrial relations revolution. It advocates the need for management, and those imbued with the business ethic, to adopt a confrontationist stance in order to change the nature of power relations in industry. Conflict is the vehicle for the society's desired changes. While several members of the society have expressed the view that there is no inherent conflict of interest between workers and employers, Hyde relates that he and a group of shop stewards at a Trade Union Training Authority course could not agree over whether unions and workers have different goals and objectives from employers. He said:

I found it almost impossible to communicate. I did not accept their basic premises and they did not accept mine. In particular they did not agree with me that bosses and workers had common interests ... Because we could not agree on fundamentals what I had to say had no relevance to them (*Arbitration*, p. 170).

Gutman, in claiming that 'the relationship between employers and employees is basically co-operative', also noted that they have 'opposing interests' and advocates the need 'for machinery for settling the inevitable disputes' which occur (*Arbitration*, pp. 306, 308).

The society is somewhat confused about the issue of conflict. It preaches the need for an increase in the level and intensity of conflict as a means to end conflict for all time; it believes that consensus can be achieved at the workplace — if unions, and their leaders, and industrial tribunals would only disappear; but it fails to appreciate that conflict is an ever-present feature of any social system where persons exercise power and authority over others. As Kemp has pointed out:

The ideology of 'consensus' fails to pay adequate recognition to the fact that there can be no resolution of institutional tensions. There can only be the transference of conflict to other institutional settings. The attitudes expressed in conflict may change, and the rules by which conflict is conducted may be altered, but conflict is inevitable in a system of multiple decision takers seeking to reduce uncertainty by control over others (Kemp, 1983, p. 219).

That there is a split between the leadership and the membership of unions — that leaders are more militant than and do not represent the interests of the members on the shopfloor — is one of the society's key assumptions. Accordingly it is believed that if and when an industrial dispute occurs, rank and file unionists would rather continue working than join the union leadership in striking against the employer. To the extent that the strike adversely affects the economic interests of the employer, the employer can make use of common law remedies to order the union to desist from such action and/or award damages which could have the associated effect of financially crippling the union concerned.

The South East Queesland Electricity Board, Mudginberri, and Dollar Sweets disputes were consistent with this analysis. In all three disputes a number of workers were prepared to accept work on the employer's terms, notwithstanding the objections and protests of union leaders and other union members. In the South East Queensland Electricity Board dispute the Queensland government introduced a number of legislative changes which played a significant part in defeating the union (Davis, 1985; Guille, 1985; McCarthy, 1985); sections 45D and 45E of the Trade Practices Act, which outlaw secondary boycotts, were used by the employer in the Mudginberri dispute; and common law remedies before the Victorian Supreme Court were used in the Dollar Sweets dispute (Mitchell, 1986).

In the Robe River dispute Peko-Wallsend hoped that its lock-out similarly would result in a split between the leadership and membership of the various unions concerned, and that once some workers had agreed to work with Peko-Wallsend, legal remedies could be used against the unions as they had been previously employed in Mudginberri and Dollar Sweets (Williams, 1986a). The strategy, however, proved to be unsuccessful. Peko-Wallsend underestimated the unions' solidarity, and the unions' tactic of seeking resolution of the dispute before the Western Australian Industrial Commission proved to be successful.

The H. R. Nicholls Society wishes to introduce legislative changes that enable 'any group of enterprise or industry employees who wish to do so to form their own union'. The legislation, the society believes, should require unions to set aside sums of money to enable rank and file members to contest union elections (Costello, 1986). Such 'reforms' (see Chapter 4) are designed to encourage faction fighting and exacerbate unions' internal tensions. The society appears to be unaware of the extensive legislation governing the internal affairs of unions (Creighton, Ford, and Mitchell, 1983, Chapters 25—30) and the faction fighting between competing elites (usually between rival federal and state branches) that has been a continuing feature of union life in Australia (McCallum, 1984).

A CLUB OR A LEAGUE?

In developing their critique of the existing industrial relations system the H. R. Nicholls Society has made much use of the 'Industrial Relations Club' concept. The term was afforded prominence after an article by Henderson in 1983, though McGuinness claims that the term was originally used by the *Australian Financial Review* (McGuinness, 1985). The Industrial Relations Club referred to by the society is the alliance, as the society sees it, comprising the Conciliation and Arbitration Commission, the ACTU, the CAI, and the Commonwealth Department of Employment and Industrial Relations, which seeks to resolve disputes by bargaining, negotiation, and compromise. The society's main criticism of the club is that decisions are not made 'according to tough-minded economic criteria' (Henderson, 1983, p. 29). This, of course, assumes that Australia's economic problems are caused by the labour market. There is little or no consideration of the possibility that Australia's economic performance is more dependent on the international economy, on government fiscal and monetary policies, on product and money markets, and so on.

Henderson's perception of a cosy, almost corporatist, club can be contrasted with Chipman's claim that 'the industrial relations area is essentially a Hobbesian State of nature which somehow subsists within an otherwise civilised society' (Hyde and Nurick, 1985, p. 124). It should also be noted that Henderson believes that the Industrial Relations Club 'has little to show for its efforts' and that 'within the Club there are internal divisions, conflict and competing interests' (Henderson, 1983, pp. 26, 23—4).

Furthermore, while Henderson may be correct in stating that 'what divides Club members is of less significance than the ... ethos that unites them' (Henderson, 1983, p. 24), clubs are often racked by what sociologists and behavioural scientists describe as intra-organizational conflict. As anyone who has been a member of a club or organization knows, individuals and groups continually struggle with each other,[12] endeavouring to enhance their power and authority. Stremski (1986), for example, documents a series of disputes and clashes within the Collingwood Football Club, by some standards *the* club in Australia! In the struggle for control of the club, various philosophies of football management, coaching, and playing have met head-on. Players have wrangled with the club over pay, have fallen in and out with rival administrations and coaches, and have disagreed among themselves about captaincy and field positions.

Henderson focused on what might be called the peak, federal-level 'club', but myriad 'industrial relations clubs' can be identified. Gutman, for example, describes himself — and by implication the society — as belonging to the 'Anti-Industrial Relations Club' (*Arbitration*, p. 300). Carmody (*Arbitration*, Chapter 10), in examining the determination of penalty rates for Saturday afternoon trading in the retail industry in New South Wales, provides information on what might be described as the 'New South Wales Industrial Relations Club' and highlights differences which have emerged among members of the Industrial Commission of New South Wales. Spry's (*Arbitration*, Chapter 5) recommendations concerning the strengthening of the federal government's industrial relations powers recognize and seek to abolish the various state 'industrial relations clubs'.

The notion of *the* Industrial Relations Club above all over-simplifies Australian industrial relations. Beside the numerous institutions/pressure groups/actors involved in industrial relations — unions/workers, employers/management/capital, governments governmental regulatory agencies courts — industrial relations manifests at many levels, including federal, state, industry, firm, enterprise, and shopfloor level. Not only is there conflict within each 'club' over allocation of power and authority, and appropriate goals and tactics, but also 'clubs' are engaged

in continual conflict and competition with each other, exper-
imenting with and developing new and different strategies,
changing and shifting alliances, as they scramble for their
respective places in the industrial relations sun. If a term is at
all useful here, then 'league' would seem to be more apposite
than 'club'; Australian industrial relations is like a league
comprising a large number and variety of competing teams.

Henderson, in developing the 'Industrial Relations Club'
notion, has abstracted industrial relations from the totality of
Australian economic, political, and social life. Many of the clubs
within the industrial relations 'league' will also belong to several
of numerous other leagues — for example the 'media league',
the 'legal league', the 'agricultural league'. Not only is there
conflict and competition within the 'industrial relations league',
but also it is involved in competition and conflict with all of the
other leagues in the 'superleague', Australia.

ROLE OF INDUSTRIAL TRIBUNALS

The H. R. Nicholls Society holds arbitration in contempt, but
their understanding of the position and role of industrial tribunals
is confused and contradictory. They have found it difficult to
discern whether industrial tribunals are followers or leaders.
Stone, for example, has alternately referred to the personnel of
industrial tribunals as 'latter-day arbitral Hitlers' (Stone, 1984a,
p. 14) and as 'conciliators leaning generally in that direction
where they discern the greater power to reside' (Stone, 1985b,
p. 24). He has industrial tribunals both dictating and being
passive agents vis-à-vis industrial-relations parties. To complicate the issue further Houlihan has praised the Conciliation and
Arbitration Commission for 'the strength' it displayed in standing
up to the meatworkers in the Mudginberri dispute. He also
observed that

The one consistent feature of the Commission's behaviour has been that
it always wants to find in favour of the side that it considers will win
the dispute ... the Arbitration Commission ... is an institution imbued
with a desire to sustain and continue itself, and the inherent pragmatism
of the institution must be used to our advantage (*Arbitration*, p. 100).

However, undoubtedly the prime example of confusion over the role of industrial tribunals is provided by McGuinness, who has developed four alternative versions of the nature and processes of industrial relations (McGuinness, 1985, pp. 2, 19, 27, 16). He has claimed firstly that the commission has established the pattern of 'strike first, arbitrate afterwards'. He claims secondly that 'the common course of events now follows a sequence of initial claim ... rejection with little discussion by the employers, strike then arbitration and finally some effort at conciliation'. McGuinness thirdly changes the sequence of events, claiming that 'arbitration is often the first stage in contemporary Australian industrial disputes, being followed by strike activity, conciliation and eventually collective bargaining'. McGuinness fourthly states that 'Most matters are settled on a fairly amicable basis, over a beer or two in the corner pub or at the club.'

At this point the incidence and level of industrial disputation in Australia deserves examination. Table 6.1 provides information on the number of disputes, workers involved, total working days lost, and working days lost per employee in the period 1970−86. The table shows that the level of industrial disputation reached a peak in the mid and late 1970s and declined significantly in the 1980s: 2900 in 1981, and 1700 in 1986. The number of workers involved in disputes has ranged from a high of 2.2 million in 1976 to fewer than half a million in 1983. Total working days lost has ranged from a high of 6.3 million in 1974 to a low of 1.3 million in 1985. The highest number of days lost per employee was 1.320 in 1974, compared to a low of 0.230 in 1985. In the period 1970−86 the average time spent on industrial disputes per employee was 0.557 days per year. Assuming a working year of 226 days (Steinke, 1983) each employee in the period 1970−85 spent 0.246 per cent of the time available for work in industrial disputes. It should also be noted that Australia has a pattern of short, sharp strikes. Between 40 and 50 per cent of disputes are resolved in one day, with between 70 and 80 per cent resolved within three days.

It is interesting to note that Henderson has suggested that 'employers should be encouraged to offer their workers a "non-strike" end of year bonus' (Henderson, 1983, p. 29). Assuming a

Table 6.1   Industrial Disputes in Australia, 1970−86

Year	Number of Disputes	Workers Involved Directly and Indirectly (Thousands)	Working Days Lost (Thousands)	Working Days Lost Per Employee
1970	2738	1367.4	2393.7	0.555
1971	2404	1326.5	3068.6	0.693
1972	2298	1113.8	2010.3	0.449
1973	2538	803.0	2634.7	0.570
1974	2809	2004.8	6292.5	1.320
1975	2432	1398.0	3509.9	0.742
1976	2055	2189.9	3799.2	0.803
1977	2090	596.2	1654.8	0.350
1978	2277	1075.6	2130.8	0.432
1979	2042	1862.9	3964.4	0.785
1980	2429	1172.6	3319.7	0.649
1981	2915	1247.2	4189.3	0.797
1982	2060	706.1	1980.4	0.358
1983	1787	470.2	1641.4	0.249
1984	1965	560.3	1370.4	0.248
1985	1845	570.5	1256.2	0.228
1986	1687	675.9	1390.7	0.242

Sources: Australian Bureau of Statistics, *Labour Reports*, Ref. No. 6.6, and *Industrial Disputes* (monthly summaries − Catalogue No. 6321.0; quarterly summaries − Catalogue No. 6322.0).

workforce of almost seven million, and given that workers are involved in disputes only once a year, many employers would probably experience financial problems in paying the bonus and/or would see little need for it, as only a small percentage of the workforce actually become involved in industrial disputes (also would 'passive' workers be encouraged to strike so that they could receive a no-strike bonus for not striking?).

It has been estimated that for the latter part of the 1970s industrial disputes constituted 5.5 per cent of temporary, non-approved absences from work. Industrial accidents (excluding

Year	Negotiation	Mediation	State Legislation or Intervention	Federal Legislation or Intervention[b]	Resumption without Negotiation	Other Methods
1970	26.3	0.7	6.5	7.2	59.2	—
1971	22.8	0.7	7.3	8.4	60.8	—
1972	22.7	1.2	9.9	7.7	58.6	—
1973	32.1	1.0	10.8	8.6	47.5	—
1974	30.7	0.2	11.6	9.2	48.1	0.1
1975	27.6	0.5	9.2	9.2	53.2	0.3
1976	27.7	0.6	11.6	10.8	48.8	0.2
1977	22.5	0.6	10.0	9.0	57.6	0.1
1978	21.0	0.5	8.7	7.4	62.3	—
1979	20.1	0.4	5.0	5.6	68.7	0.1
1980	21.4	0.6	5.4	7.5[b]	64.9	0.2
1981	22.3	0.5	7.5	7.5[b]	61.7	0.5
1982	22.8	a	5.9	6.2[b]	64.7	0.4
1983	22.8	a	7.4	5.7[b]	63.1	1.1
1984	21.1	a	6.8	5.9[b]	65.0	1.2
1985	17.8	a	6.2	10.1[b]	64.0	1.9

Sources: Australian Bureau of Statistics, *Labour Reports* Ref. No. 6.6, and *Industrial Disputes* (quarterly summaries — Catalogue No. 6322.0).

[a] Information no longer supplied
[b] From 1980 should read as federal and joint federal–state legislation and intervention.

industrial deaths, which have been estimated at 400 per year) accounted for 6.3 per cent of absences; off-the-job accidents, 12 per cent; drug and alcohol abuse, 18 per cent; the 'sickie', 19 per cent; and general illness, 39 per cent (Crawford and Volard, 1981). Despite the H. R. Nicholls Society's concern about productivity and efficiency, it has been silent on the problems of industrial and occupational health and safety, or improvements in general health and the associated problems of drug and alcohol dependence.

Table 6.2 provides information on the method of settling disputes in Australia in the period 1970–85. The table shows that almost 60 per cent of disputes ended in a resumption of work without negotiation; the workforce simply returned to work after either 'going out on the grass' or attending a stopwork meeting. Approximately 25 per cent of disputes were resolved by negotiation or collective bargaining with approximately 15 per cent being resolved by either state or federal industrial tribunals. The most interesting thing about Table 6.2 is the relatively small percentage of disputes resolved by industrial tribunals, casting serious doubt on Gutman's claim that 'the inclination of many managers [is] to dump their industrial relations problems as speedily as possible on the doorstep of industrial tribunals' (Gutman, 1986, p. 58).

The H. R. Nicholls Society sees industrial tribunals as 'captured' by unions (see Theories of Regulation, Chapter 1). Scherer's article 'State Syndicalism?' (Hyde and Nurick, 1985, Chapter 6) has become seminal among the society's membership. Scherer adopted the *Shorter Oxford Dictionary* definition of syndicalism:

a movement among industrial workers having as its object the transfer of the means of production and distribution from their present owners to unions of workers for the benefit of the workers, the method generally favoured for the accomplishment of this being the general strike.

Scherer argued that 'the arbitral tribunals ... can be described as the executive committee of the labour movement' and that 'It is no great revelation to observe that union principles have "captured" the arbitration tribunals' (Hyde and Nurick, 1985, p. 94).

Apart from a few radical elements, such as the Industrial Workers of the World in the early part of this century, Australian unions do not fit the syndicalism tradition. Australian unions have linked their development to the fortunes of Australian capitalism and have sought to protect and advance the rights and interests of members by combining elements of industrial relations: direct negotiations with employers, politics, and conciliation and arbitration (Nairn, 1973; Martin, 1980; Dabscheck and Niland, 1981; Hagan, 1981). The general strike — with the exception of the unsuccessful national, 24-hour strike against the Fraser coalition government's changes to Medibank in 1976 — has not been 'the method generally favoured' by Australian unions to gain desired objectives.

While industrial tribunals have from time to time appeared to endorse or adopt union principles and ideas, at other times they have adopted ideas and concepts developed by employers. Employers, for example, have been successful before tribunals in gaining acceptance of the 'capacity to pay principle', the end of automatic quarterly cost of living adjustments, in 1953, the introduction of the total wage, in 1967, and endorsement of the importance of 'management prerogatives'. Interestingly 'management prerogatives' might be used as a subject heading for the following quote from Higgins, the H. R. Nicholls Society's bête noire:

The Court leaves every employer free to carry on the business of his own system, so long as he does not perpetuate industrial trouble or endanger industrial peace; free to choose his employees on their merits and according to his exigencies; free to make use of new machines, of improved methods, of financial advantages, of advantages of locality, of superior knowledge; free to put the utmost pressure on anything and everything except human life (Higgins, 1915, p. 21).

In the real world of industrial relations, tribunals hand down decisions which sometimes favour employers, sometimes favour unions, and sometimes upset both parties, as well as the government of the day. In the 1953 *Basic Wage Inquiry* the then Arbitration Court pointed out that 'It is really impossible to settle a dispute in a way that satisfies all parties, it is frequently impossible to arrive at a just settlement which satisfies even one of the parties to the dispute' (77 CAR 477, p. 507). Scherer and the H. R. Nicholls Society have not addressed the issue of how it can be possible that industrial tribunals are first captured by one group of parties, then by an opposing group of parties.

Some writers have viewed the power relationship between industrial tribunals and unions as the inverse of that suggested by Scherer. Both Blackburn (1940) and Howard (1977), for example, have perceived unions as becoming overly dependent and reliant on industrial tribunals, reducing their ability to adequately represent the needs and interests of members. Howard goes so far as to argue that Australian unions are 'industrial cosmetics', being 'a labour movement in form and intention rather than in tactic and achievement' (1977, pp. 269—70).

Industrial tribunals are not the passive instruments Scherer implies. Their personnel have continually asserted that they are independent of the government of the day as well as the parties to disputes and have developed their own ideas and experimented with new programmes. Higgins's 'a new province for law and order', the 10 per cent cut in the basic wage in 1931, Kelly's ending of the automatic quarterly cost of living adjustments in 1953, Kirby's accommodating approach in the 1960s and 1970s, and Sir John Moore's wage indexation experiments have all been attempts by strong and independent arbitrators to respond to the industrial relations and economic problems of their respective eras.

It could be argued that in developing such schemes the arbitrators attempted to do the capturing, seeking to convince parties of the wisdom of following the tribunal's lead down a desired path of industrial relations regulation. As discussed in Chapter 1, industrial tribunals are in a bargaining relationship with the parties. The tribunals perform a complex balancing act as they juggle competing claims and interests *and* balance the parties' expectations against their own interpretations of regulation.

COURTS AND TRIBUNALS

Common law contracts are the H. R. Nicholls Society's preferred means of regulating employment relationships. Industrial tribunals' lack of enforcement powers makes them seriously flawed, in the society's view. The attraction of common law, and for that matter sections 45D and 45E of the Trade Practices Act, is that unions and workers can be sued for damages in the event of a strike or breach of contract. However, industrial tribunals limit recourse to common law. As Mitchell has pointed out, 'A court of equity will not usually grant an injunction when there is an alternative tribunal which has the authority to deal with the dispute between the parties' (1976, p. 457). If, however, conciliation and arbitration avenues are exhausted, common law actions may proceed, followed by awarding of damages.[13]

As indicated at Table 6.2, industrial disputes are generally resolved by the processes of bargaining, conciliation, and arbitration. As a dispute continues, the costs associated with the dispute — what economists refer to as 'the costs of disagreeing' — increase, which provides an incentive for all parties (both sides) to offer compromises and eventually end the dispute. The availability of common law and damages awards has the potential to alter this fundamentally.

If one party (the employer, say) knows or believes that the equity courts will order the other party (the union(s), say) to compensate them for dispute-related economic losses, the first party's incentive to resolve the dispute through the processes of bargaining and negotiation will be substantially reduced. In addition, the potential availability of common law remedies may thwart the attempts of third-party neutrals to resolve the dispute through the processes of conciliation and arbitration. In this sense, then, it could be argued that the existence and availability of common law has the potential to undermine and frustrate the use of industrial tribunals in regulating industrial relations in Australia.[14]

Could a party that received financial support from external sources — particularly sources that expressed a desire to abolish industrial tribunals — to tide them over while waiting for an equity court to award them common law damages in fact be involved in a conspiracy (or tort) to thwart the processes of conciliation and arbitration and the operation of industrial tribunals? It should not be forgotten that industrial tribunals are legislatively established and sanctioned. Opposing groups would almost certainly experiment with and develop countervailing common law remedies and defences. Unions, for example, could investigate the use of torts for conspiracy against employers for their non-preparedness to make use of industrial tribunals, developing defences of their rights in the face of 'a deliberate fomentation of trouble by anti-unionists or breakaway unionists' (Mitchell, 1976, p. 457).

Unions could conceivably develop defences based on International Labour Organisation conventions that have been ratified by Australia under the external affairs power of the Constitution. The two relevant conventions are *Freedom of Association and Protection of the Right to Organise*, number 87, and *Right to Organise and Collective Bargaining*, number 98. A section of convention number 98 states that

Workers and employers' organisations shall enjoy adequate protection against any acts of interference by each other or each other's agents or members in their establishment, functioning or administration. Acts which are designed to promote the establishment of workers' organisations under the control of employers shall be deemed to constitute acts of interference (DEIR, 1985, Convention No. 98).

In its focusing on the enforcement and damage aspects of breaches of contract, the H. R. Nicholls Society has ignored how agreements are reached or made. It appears to be unaware of the traditional industrial relations distinction between interest and rights disputes — that is, the difference between making and interpreting agreements. Under labour law in the United States, interest disputes are not subject to common law remedies. Strikes and lockouts are basic tactics that the parties can make use of as they negotiate a contract; the major obligation of the parties is to bargain in good faith. Breaches of an agreement, once it has been made, are subject to legal remedies.[15] The major disputes associated with the New Right — South East Queensland Electricity Board, Mudginberri, Dollar Sweets, and Robe River — have been interest disputes rather than rights disputes. They were all attempts to negotiate a new agreement/award, rather than being breaches of contract. If American labour law is used as a model, common law actions are not applicable.

Gutman, in criticizing industrial tribunals and arguing for increased reliance on common law, has maintained that

Industrial relations disputes are more like commercial bargaining or international negotiations where, as long as neither party is under duress, only the parties themselves can trade concessions and, by give and take, eventually arrive at agreements which are beneficial to both. Judicial processes have no useful role to play in such negotiations which should be settled freely between the parties (*Arbitration*, p. 307).

The view that 'judicial processes have no useful role to play' is at odds with the H. R. Nicholls Society's advocacy of reliance on common law enforcement and damage powers, and the condemning of industrial tribunals because of their lack of such powers. In addition, both Gutman and the H. R. Nicholls Society seem to be unaware of recent developments in Australian commercial law, which is moving away from a reliance on courts to what have loosely been described as alternative dispute-resolution procedures.

In September 1986 the Commonwealth Department of the Attorney-General issued a set of papers, *Dispute Resolution in Commercial Matters*. The papers express concern about the costs and delays associated with court cases, and the damage that such cases may do to long-lived relationships between commercial parties. As Mr Justice Rogers of the Supreme Court of New South Wales said, 'a court is unable to deal with the matters which may be the underlying and fundamental causes of the dispute between the parties' (Attorney-General, 1986, p. 64). The alternative dispute-resolution procedures that are nowadays being utilized and suggested make use of mediation, umpires, and arbitration. While being applied in the arena favoured by the H. R. Nicholls Society they remain close to the industrial relations tradition that the society, by its very existence, vilifies.

REAPPEARANCE OF THE INVISIBLE HAND

The H. R. Nicholls Society believes that the various problems of the Australian economy would be rectified if government regulation and interference with the operation of the market were brought to an end. It regards the market as the best arbiter of people's desires and needs. The market provides individuals with incentives, is flexible , enhances efficiency, and is the source of economic growth. The market encourages competition, which in turn enables the best and most efficient to survive and prosper. The market is monitored by prices; changes in prices act as signals, reflecting changes in consumer tastes, and reallocate resources, from less to more efficient sectors of the economy.

A major criticism the society brings to its argument against market interference (apart from general economic problems) is the level of youth unemployment (Hyde and Nurick, 1985, Chapter 7; Stone 1985a; *Arbitration*, Chapter 9). Youth unemployment, according to the society, dramatically illustrates the harmful effects of the minimum-wage policies of industrial tribunals. It maintains that if youth wages were allowed to fall, employers would have an incentive to employ greater numbers of young people. Two criticisms of these views of youth unemployment can be made; one is theoretical, the other empirical.

First, the prices role is crucial to the H. R. Nicholls Society argument. In traditional neo-classical analysis, prices reflect the total value of a transaction to both the buyer and the seller. A problem that haunts economic neo-classicists is that elements besides price may be involved in a transaction. For example, economic agents can indulge in non-price forms of competition — quality, reliability of service, discrimination (favouritism), and so on. Adam Smith, whose 'invisible hand' guides the society, observed that workers evaluated jobs in terms of not only wages but also the agreeableness or disagreeableness associated with the work concerned. Given the variability of tastes among individuals it is possible to conceive of many combinations of price and non-price aspects of a transaction that would afford the same outcome of a transaction. In addition, traditional neo-classical economics views markets as being akin to an auction, where markets instantaneously clear, with buyers and sellers having an intermittent, short-term, and impersonal relationship. The possibility of those in the market having a longer term, continuing, or subjective relationship is ignored. Many transactions, particularly those in the labour market, are characterized by long-term relationships.[16]

In discussing youth unemployment, Porter, the H. R. Nicholls Society's leading economist, has expressed some reservation about wages as a reflection of value for both the supply and demand sides of the market. On the supply side he considers it necessary to 'start to think of the earnings of young people in a much broader light, with the total "wage" as valued by the recipient being equal to the sum of the monetary wage payment plus the net value of the training given' (*Arbitration*, pp. 214–15). Porter's argument is that for young people a job not only provides them with a wage and income now but also provides them with training (or the acquisition of human capital) that enhances lifetime employment and income. The training component of youth employment is an additional benefit which, Porter believes, needs to be incorporated into discussions of youth unemployment. Putting to one side the problem of actually measuring this training component, Porter is postulating that employed young people are being overpaid, or receiving 'rent', because of the existence of the training component that enhances lifetime employment and income. Youth wages could be lowered because of the presumptive training component, which in turn would enable more, lower priced young people to obtain employment.

When Porter examines the demand side of the market, however, it is apparent that lower wages would not necessarily result in an increase in employment levels for young people, because of the phenomenon of 'lemons'. He points out

that special schemes to announce the cheapest car, the deepest discount computer, or the lowest wage worker, as a way of promoting demand, will not work if these very low prices are themselves taken as an indicator of low quality ... A poor employee can readily undermine worker morale, can damage equipment and upset customers. The firm's insurance, and notably workmen's compensation rating, can deteriorate with the introduction of a slack or irresponsible worker or group of workers, and these considerations may often make employers unwilling to take on any but the most (apparently) reliable workers (*Arbitration*, p. 221).

In short, the price of labour is used as a proxy for quality, and low wages, rather than encouraging employment as predicted by neo-classical economics, discourage employment. More generally, the problem for the H. R. Nicholls Society is that the problems associated with the use of prices as an allocative mechanism reduce the efficacy of its call for total reliance on market mechanisms and the abolition or reduction of governmental regulation.

Since the society strongly supports the deregulatory policies pursued by the British Thatcher government and America's Reagan administration, rates of youth unemployment in Australia, America, and Great Britain deserve comparison. Additionally both the United States and Great Britain are regarded as collective bargaining countries, whereas Australia makes extensive use of industrial tribunals. The relative efficacy of the regulated and deregulated labour markets may therefore be tested by means of the youth unemployment comparison.

Table 6.3 provides information on total and youth unemployment for Australia, America, and Great Britain for the period April 1981 to October 1986. Each country collects and collates its data on youth unemployment in different ways. Australia looks at 15–19-year-olds; America, 16–19-year-olds; Great Britain persons under 18, and 18–19-year-olds. The British have changed their data-collection method twice in the period, and unemployment levels are therefore understated by comparison with earlier series. It should also be noted that while Australia's school leavers inflate the figures at the end of the calendar year, the same phenomenon occurs in the other two countries in the middle of the year. Data for April and October have been gathered in an attempt to overcome or reduce this problem.

Table 6.3 shows that America and Great Britain have youth unemployment problems similar to Australia's. Between April 1981 and April 1983 Australia fared better than America; since then the American performance has generally speaking been better than Australia's. Except for the under-18-category in April 1984 and April 1985, Great Britain has had a consistently poorer record than Australia. The rates of youth unemployment as a ratio of total unemployment for Australia, America, and Great Britain are (approximately) 2.3, 2.5, and 1.8 respectively. Youth unemployment is a problem common to all three countries despite and not because of differences in the approach to labour-market regulation.

Table 6.3 Total and Teenage Unemployment Rates (Percentage) for Australia, the United States, and Great Britain, April 1981–October 1986

| | | Australia | | United States | | Great Britain | |
		Total	15–19	Total	16–19	Total	Under 18	18–19
1981	Apr.	5.6	14.4	7.0	18.2	10.3	16.1	18.3
	Oct.	5.5	14.8	7.5	20.1	12.2	27.8	22.3
1982	Apr.	6.4	16.6	9.2	22.3	12.3	22.1	22.5
	Oct.	7.7	18.1	9.9	23.7	12.6[a]	27.1[a]	24.6[a]
1983	Apr.	10.2	23.0	10.0	23.0	13.2	24.6	25.3
	Oct.	9.3	22.1	8.4	21.4	12.9	26.0	26.9
1984	Apr.	9.5	20.5	7.6	18.6	12.8	16.8	26.4
	Oct.	8.4	20.0	7.0	18.5	13.3	22.8	28.8
1985	Apr.	9.2	19.9	7.1	16.9	13.5	16.8	25.5
	Oct.	7.9	17.5	6.8	20.0	13.5	21.0	25.1
1986	Apr.	8.0	19.4	7.1	19.6	12.3[b]	21.8[b]	21.1[b]
	Oct.	7.8	17.9	7.0	17.6	11.7	21.8	20.2

Sources: Australian Bureau of Statistics, *The Labour Force — Australia*, Catalogue No. 6203.0; US Department of Labor, *Bureau of Labor Statistics*; (UK) Department of Employment, *Employment Gazette*.

[a] new series; [b] new series

CONCLUSION

It should not be surprising that during periods of economic adversity different groups will compete and offer different solutions. While some have advocated industrial relations approaches based on co-operation and a preparedness to work through existing institutional arrangements, others have advocated a more aggressive or a confrontationist approach for Australia in the 1980s.

The H. R. Nicholls Society represents a new force in Australian industrial relations. While it has experienced some success in the past, and may have more in the future, one should be wary of overstating its role and influence. Notwithstanding its belief in the efficacy of the 'invisible hand' in the market-place, and its concomitant anxiety over government intervention, the society stresses the importance of the process of the law and of strong government.

The society preaches confrontation and conflict in the search for utopia. It believes that industrial conflict will simply disappear once unions are controlled and the current institutions for conflict resolution are abolished, failing to realize that such a policy itself generates conflict and that conflict is and always will be a feature of the world of work. The society offers a 'final solution' and then a 'big bang'. Its fundamental problem, however, is the 'fall-out' that many associate with the big-bang creation of what Henry Bournes Higgins, in the early part of this century, called 'a new province for law and order'.

NOTES

1 For example see Williams 1986a and the *Sydney Morning Herald* and the *Australian*, 6 September 1986.

2 See the *Australian Financial Review*, 29 August 1986. For another example of Hawke's views concerning the New Right see the *Australian*, 12 December 1986.

3 See the *Australian Financial Review*, the *Sydney Morning Herald*, and the *Australian*, 7 October 1986.

4 See the *Sydney Morning Herald* and the *Australian*, 1 December 1986. For similar views expressed by Macphee see the *Sydney Morning Herald*, 3 September 1986. For a more general exposition of this version of liberalism see Thompson, Brandis, and Harley (1986).

5 For other accounts of Powell's views see the *Sydney Morning Herald*, 2 October 1986, and the *Australian Financial Review* and the *Australian*, 2 and 3 October 1986.

6 It should, however, be noted that there have been a few disparaging references to left wing ideas and officials within unions. See Davis (1985), Stone (1985a, 1986), and Leard (1986).

7 Evans seems to be unaware that his hero H. R. Nicholls has said that 'differences of opinion do not count for much, but differences of conduct are everything. We may agree to differ, but if we once lose the gentlemanly conduct in doing it, and not doing things because it is not right to do them, we are on a downward path, and the result leads to a great deal of misconception and mischief' (*Arbitration*, p. 347).

8 The *Harvester* case was heard under the 1906 Excise Tariff Act. Even though the High Court held it to be unconstitutional, Higgins applied the Harvester decision in preventing and settling disputes under the 1904 Conciliation and Arbitration Act.

9 For a more general discussion of the ideology of the New Right in Australia see Sawer (1982) and Coghill (1987).

10 In the early 1950s the Menzies coalition government began conducting 'negotiations with the trade union movement solely through the ACTU' (Martin, 1958, p. 41), despite non-affiliation of the Australian Workers Union, the ACTU's traditional rival (until affiliation in 1967), and the existence of rival white collar and public sector peak-union bodies. This had the effect of increasing the stature and role of the ACTU both within and outside the trade union movement.

11 For a further discussion of the relationship between employers/ business and the Hawke government see Singleton (1985), Stewart (1985), McEachern (1985, 1986), and Gerritsen (1986).

12 Henderson apparently had an unhappy time as a member of the club. See *Arbitration*, Chapter 11.

13 It should be noted that legislation in South Australia in 1984 — section 143A of the Industrial Conciliation and Arbitration Act — places general restrictions on the use of torts for industrial disputes.

14 For a fuller discussion of these ideas see Mitchell (1986).

15 For further discussion of the nuances of American industrial relations see Kochan (1980).

16 For an extensive critique of neo-classical economics see Thurow (1983), especially Chapter 1.

CHAPTER 7

Groping in the Dark

Undoubtedly the major industrial relations event in Australia in 1987 was the introduction of the two-tiered system, described in Chapter 5. In combining centralization and decentralization the two-tiered system sought to enhance microeconomic efficiency in the interests of better overall economic performance, following the balance of payments problems experienced by Australia in 1985 and 1986. The introduction of the two-tiered system in 1987 was also noteworthy because of the emergence of three major reform proposals. First, there was the Hawke government's long-awaited response to the Hancock Report, enshrined in the 1987 Industrial Relations Bill. Second, the Australian Council of Trade Unions (ACTU) and the Trade Development Council (TDC) issued *Australia Reconstructed*, which developed yet another corporatist blueprint in response to the problems of the economy. Third, a Constitutional Commission created by the Hawke government issued a series of reports proposing changes to the Australian Constitution which, if passed, could have significant industrial relations implications. Each of these reform proposals will be examined in turn.

INDUSTRIAL RELATIONS BILL, 1987

On 14 May 1987 the Commonwealth Minister for Employment and Industrial Relations, Ralph Willis, introduced an Industrial Relations Bill in the House of Representatives. In the second reading speech Willis told Parliament that while the Bill was based on the 1985 Hancock Report (see Chapter 4), 'it is by no means a faithful legislative replica of the Report. Indeed, some key recommendations of the Report have been rejected, whilst others have been substantially varied' (Willis, 1987, p. 4). Like the Hancock Report the Bill sought greater co-operation with the states, enabling members of the Australian Conciliation and Arbitration Commission to exercise powers under state laws; joint proceedings and conferences; and greater co-operation between Commonwealth and state authorities (clauses 202–7).

The Bill also followed the Hancock Report in recommending the Australian Industrial Relations Commission, to replace the Conciliation and Arbitration Commission; the Australian Labour Court, to replace the Industrial Division of the Federal Court of Australia; and the dual appointment of legally qualified deputy presidential members of the proposed commission to the Labour Court. Unlike the Hancock Report, however, the Bill rejected the idea of the same person being president of the proposed commission and chief judge of the Labour Court; it also opposed the appointment of a vice-president to the proposed commission. The Bill envisaged that the Labour Court would comprise the sole jurisdiction of both its judges and the dually appointed deputy presidential members of the proposed commission. Given the 1956 *Boilermakers* case, the constitutionality of the changes was, it seems, what the Bill was addressing in proposing these two types of appointees: if a High Court challenge was successful, it was conceivable that not all the members of the Labour Court would have their commissions terminated.[1]

The Bill followed the Hancock Report in seeking to reduce the number of Australian unions. The Bill sought to encourage the amalgamation of unions on industry lines (clauses 263–80), to increase the minimum membership of unions seeking registration from 100 to 1000 (clause 219), and regularly to review the registration of unions already registered with fewer than 1000 members (clause 223). As Chapter 4 has argued, these provisions would be unlikely to reduce the number of Australian unions substantially as most small unions are registered at the state rather than the federal level (see Table 4.1).

Other interesting features of the Bill included procedures to enable the proposed commission to encourage the inclusion of grievance procedures in awards (clauses 122, 123), enabling presidential members to hear demarcation disputes (clause 148), post-dispute review procedures (clause 162), and power for the proposed commission to hear unfair dismissal cases (clause 188).

Enforcement and compliance was a major area in which the Bill differed from the Hancock Report. Other than deregistration of unions the Hancock Report eschewed sanctions and offered no recommendations concerning secondary boycotts, because of differences on this issue among members of the Hancock Committee. The Bill, on the other hand, contained enforcement and compliance provisions that produced a storm of protest and controversy and ultimately caused scuttling of the Bill.

In his second reading speech to Parliament, Willis said:

> The Government believes that the tribunals established by this Bill should have complete authority to ensure adherence by the parties within the federal industrial relations system to the standards applying under that system. It is considered that the availability of other forms of legal remedies from state courts or under state laws could well be damaging to the federal Commission's charter to prevent and settle industrial disputes and could interfere with its ability to perform that function, to the ulimate detriment of the parties (Willis, 1987, p. 19).

In addition he said, 'It is the intention of the legislation to ensure that where other remedies are available under any state or territory legislation or in tort that are inconsistent with the relevant federal remedies, then the federal remedies are to be paramount' (Willis, 1987, p. 22). Via section 109 of the Australian Constitution (where there is an inconsistency between a state and Commonwealth law, the Commonwealth law prevails) Willis hoped to render redundant, at the federal level at least, Sir Joh Bjelke-Petersen's government's 1987 Industrial (Commercial Practices) Act, which imposed fines of up to $250 000 for unions, and $50 000 for individuals, participating in industrial disputes in Queensland.

Clause 64 of the Bill granted the Labour Court exclusive jurisdiction over other courts with respect to enforcement. Both state equity courts and the Federal Court, with some exceptions, were precluded from becoming involved in actions pertaining to industrial disputes and secondary boycotts. Common law damages and actions under sections 45D and 45E of the Trade

Practices Act were still available; however, such matters would now be adjudicated by the Labour Court rather than equity courts.

With both industrial disputes and secondary boycotts, recourse to the Labour Court was not automatic. The Bill enabled the proposed commission to first try to resolve the dispute. If its attempts were unsuccessful, the proposed commission was empowered to issue a certificate (clauses 167, 197) which handed over the dispute to the Labour Court. In the case of an industrial dispute the Labour Court could impose fines of up to $1000 a day for an individual, and $5000 for a body corporate (a five-fold increase over the fines in the existing Conciliation and Arbitration Act), alter the membership rules of a union to exclude specified groups from membership, impose conditions on the future conduct of the union, and deregister the union (clause 215). While the Bill sought to limit tort actions in other jurisdictions, it did allow a number of important exceptions. The Bill did not exclude actions for compensatory damages, actions for injunctions to prevent physical harm to persons or property, actions in respect of conversion, detinue or defamation, proceedings for contravention of an award or direction by a state industrial tribunal, and prosecutions for offences (cause 216). The Labour Court was empowered to use all of the powers under sections 45D and 45E of the Trade Practices Act (clauses 193—8) to deal with secondary boycotts.

Employer groups and business organizations throughout Australia bitterly attacked the 1987 Industrial Relations Bill, condemning the enforcement and compliance provisions in particular. They objected to the creation of the Labour Court and to having restrictions placed on their ability to mount common law and secondary boycott actions before state equity courts and the Federal Court (while they were to be able to mount such actions before the Labour Court, they anticipated that its prospective members would not be as tough on unions as would the judges of the various equity courts).[2] Employer and business organizations also objected to the commission being granted the initial power to resolve industrial disputes and secondary boycotts, and its power to issue a certificate before the dispute could be handed over to the Labour Court (Chapter 6 shows that the practice of equity courts has been not to proceed until convinced that an industrial tribunal has exhausted attempts at resolving the dispute). The organizations feared that the granting of certificates would create delays that would impose unreasonable burdens on employers involved in disputes. The Australian Democrats, who held the balance of power in the Senate, were prepared to agree to the Bill if the Hawke government would include a time limit on the issuing of certificates. After negotiations Willis apparently agreed to a three-day limit.[3]

Employer and business organizations announced plans for a one-million-dollar advertising campaign directed against the Bill. However, before they had a chance to pursue their campaign the Hawke government did a political somersault, first announcing that it would delay the passage of the Bill and then agreeing to the deletion of the enforcement provisions opposed by the employers.

The reason for the Hawke government's about-face was that less than two weeks after Willis had introduced the Bill into Parliament the prime minister received advice from the Australian Labour Party's (ALP) professional pollsters that his government would be returned to office, for a third term, if a snap federal election was held. Hawke heeded this advice and called an election for 11 July 1987. The concerted opposition of employers and business to the 1987 Industrial Relations Bill, however, needed to be neutralized to enhance, or at least not put in jeopardy, the ALP's prospects of electoral success.

AUSTRALIA RECONSTRUCTED

Chapter 5 describes how Australia's economic problems during 1985, 1986, and 1987 resulted in the negotiation of the Accord Mark II, the abandonment of wage indexation, and the introduction of the two-tiered system. In 1986 the ACTU entered into discussions with the Commonwealth Minister for Trade, John Dawkins, concerning the possibility of sending a fact-finding mission to several Western European countries that had experienced similar economic problems to Australia's. The

ACTU was particularly 'concerned to examine those countries which had overcome balance of payments constraints in ways which produced low unemployment, low inflation and economic growth which is most equitably distributed'. The request was agreed to and a joint ACTU–TDC Mission visited Sweden, Norway, Austria, West Germany, and the United Kingdom during August and September 1986. The mission's terms of reference were

To examine the relation of government, trade unions and business and available tripartite mechanisms in the formulation and implementation of trade and related policies.
To consider the implications of technology, work organisations, education and productivity for international competitiveness.
To evaluate the contribution of trade union research, education and organisation to union participation in trade related issues (*Australia*, p. xi).

On 29 July 1987 the mission released its report under the title *Australia Reconstructed*. The report is divided into six chapters: Macroeconomic Policy; Wages, Prices, and Incomes; Trade and Industry Policy; Labour Market Policies; Industrial Democracy; and Trade Unions. Each chapter is divided into two sections: observations, and implications and recommendations (This structure has unfortunately produced some overlaps and repetition.)

Like the Accord (Mark I), the 1983 National Economic Summit Conference, and the Hancock Report before it *Australia Reconstructed* repeats the claim that 'high consensus economies generally performed better ... than did low consensus ones' (p. 13) and is particularly enamoured with, and bases most of its recommendations on, the operation and performance of corporatist policies in Sweden. *Australia Reconstructed* maintains that Australia should continue to employ a centralized system of wage determination. However, in a major departure from the Accord, the summit, the Hancock Report, and most importantly traditional ACTU policy, its authors contend that wages should be linked to productivity movements in the export- or trade-based sector of the economy (*Australia*, p. 27). It is as if *Australia Reconstructed* has adopted the wages norm of employers!

The book's continuing and overriding message is the need to enhance productivity and efficiency to bring about restructuring (reconstruction) of the economy. Increased production and wealth creation are seen as being more important than distribution of either (*Australia*, p. 154). Nevertheless the industry policy recommendations involve redistribution of resources from other sections of the economy to the manufacturing sector. Embedded in *Australia Reconstructed* is the distribution decision that manufacturing is the most important sector of the Australian economy. Virtually all of *Australia Reconstructed*'s recommendations concerning labour-market training, industrial democracy, and trade union education are designed to increase productivity and efficiency.

According to *Australia Reconstructed* the best way to achieve economic recovery and to overcome balance of payments problems is by using industry policies designed to help Australian manufacturers compete against overseas producers. A National Development Fund, to be mainly financed by a 20 per cent levy on superannuation funds, is recommended as a source of loans, on favourable terms, for carefully chosen sectors of manufacturing. Industry policy, whether based on favourable loans or Commonwealth government funds, has the appearance of being a substitute for tariff protection.

Australia Reconstructed recommends that 'the Australian trade union movement should plan to have no more than twenty union organisations within two years' (p. 190), by forming either industry-based groups or federations of large, general unions. Such rationalization of union structure is seen as achieving economies of scale, increasing the range and quality of service to members, and providing unions with more resources for research, education, and organization. These recommendations closely follow those of *Future Strategies for the Trade Union Movement*, released by the ACTU in May 1987.

The oddest or most intriguing aspect of *Australia Reconstructed* concerns its comments on enforcement, particularly in the context of the ACTU's hostility to the policies of the New Right. In examining Sweden *Australia Reconstructed* notes that

Industrial action during a contract period is illegal. In the case of an illegal strike, employers may sue the union for damages; this puts a responsibility on union officials to discourage their members from taking part. Individual union members can be fined for taking part in illegal strike action, but the fines, imposed by the Labour Court, are relatively small (p. 174).[4]

Chapter 3 examined and rejected the claim that strongly corporatist, or consensus-based, economies outperform those with less or limited degrees of corporatism or consensus. It is not clear that the Swedish model — not examined at Chapter 3 — has been as successful as is implied in *Australia Reconstructed*. Both Martin (1984, pp. 288–338) and Peterson (1985, pp. 331–4) have referred to the end or decline of the Swedish model. Hammarstrom (1987, pp. 204–5) is uncertain about the future direction of Swedish industrial relations and notes the possible development of 'fragmented bargaining structures'. Lash (1985, pp. 217, 236) has claimed that Swedish labour markets are in the process of fragmentation and 'that there is a long-term trend towards decentralisation of Swedish industrial relations'. Lash has also observed that public sector employees regard having their wages determined 'on the basis of a minority of private sector blue collar workers — despite the key role of the export industry — [as] something of an anachronism' (Lash, 1985, p. 224). The implication of this for both *Australia Reconstructed* and the ACTU is that attempting to apply a centralized norm in a decentralized manner, a norm which is mainly designed to satisfy the needs of a particular sector, could result in conflict and tensions within and between unions.

Australia Reconstructed, with its espousal of the need to enhance productivity and efficiency, the development of a wage norm based on productivity in the export sector, its radical proposals concerning union structure, and even its (apparent) countenancing of limits on the right to strike, demonstrates how deeply the economic crisis of 1985 and 1986 affected the upper echelons of the ACTU. *Australia Reconstructed* represents an attempt to confront the economic and balance of payments problems experienced by Australia. It is unlikely, however, that Australia will proceed down the path advocated. Employer organizations have expressed opposition to the thrust of its proposals (CAI, 1987)[5]. The Hawke government has been selectively pursuing industry policy since 1983[6] and is committed to labour-market training; it is unlikely, however, to establish the National Development Fund, which is at the heart of *Australia Reconstructed*'s recommendations.

HIGH COURT AND CONSTITUTIONAL CHANGE

On 19 December 1985 Lionel Bowen, the Commonwealth Attorney-General, announced the formation of a constitutional commission to consider and offer suggestions for the revision of the Australian Constitution. During 1987 various committees issued a series of reports. The recommendations that have implications for industrial relations will be considered here.

The Commonwealth government's major industrial relations power stems from section 51, paragraph xxxv, of the Constitution, which empowers it to establish industrial tribunals that can make use of conciliation and arbitration to settle and prevent interstate industrial disputes. The Commonwealth government, subject to other powers available to it, cannot directly legislate in industrial relations per se and is forced by the Constitution to delegate industrial relations powers to industrial tribunals. The High Court has assumed an important role in Australian industrial relations in its capacity of interpreting the Constitution. For example, the High Court traditionally adopted a narrow interpretation of the words 'industrial disputes', maintaining that certain types of employment were not 'industrial' in character and that disputes over managerial prerogatives were not 'industrial disputes' and hence were outside the jurisdiction of the Conciliation and Arbitration Commission.

Since 1983 the High Court has adopted a broader definition of 'industrial disputes', increasing the scope of matters that can be handled by the commission. In the *Social Welfare Union* case (47 ALR 225) the High Court ruled that the words 'industrial disputes' should 'be given their popular meaning — what they convey to the man in the street'. In a string of decisions since then the High Court has ruled that the commission has power to hear disputes over matters including technological change, redundancy and unfair dismissal, superannuation, manning and recruitment, and reinstatement (though with this last case there is a cloud over the 'interstate' question). In addition, in the *Tasmanian Dams* case (57 ALJR 450), which involved an environmental dispute between the Commonwealth and the Tasmanian governments over whether the latter could build a dam in the Tasmanian wilderness, the High Court ruled in favour of the Commonwealth government on the basis of the external affairs power of the Constitution (section 51, paragraph xxix). By being a signatory of an international treaty the Commonwealth government derived power to achieve the objects of the treaty. The importance of this decision for industrial relations is that Australia has ratified many International Labour Organisation Conventions (DEIR, 1985), and it is conceivable that if the Commonwealth government enacted appropriate legislation it could assume direct industrial relations powers. Further, given section 109 of the Constitution, Commonwealth laws could override state laws.

The Constitutional Commission committee chaired by Sir John Moore which considered *distribution of powers* recommended that section 51, paragraph xxxv, 'be deleted and replaced with a new provision giving the Commonwealth Parliament a concurrent power with the State parliaments with respect to industrial relations and employment matters'. The committee maintained that the Commonwealth government should have full powers to deal with industrial matters and quoted the need 'for the control of the rate of wage increases which the Fraser government advocated in 1982' as an example. To provide for objections to this recommendation the committee recommended that the words 'or any industrial matter in so much of an industry is covered by federal awards' be added to section 51, paragraph xxxv, to eliminate jurisdictional limitations on the operation of the commission (Constitutional Commission, 1987b, p. 35).

The *trade and national economic management committee* recommended that a new section of the Constitution be created (section 51, paragraph 1A), granting the Commonwealth government power over 'matters affecting the national economy'. In submitting this recommendation the committee claimed that the Commonwealth government experienced problems with industrial relations and the implementation of prices and incomes policies (Constitutional Commission, 1987c, pp. 24–5, 32–5). The committee also recommended that the Commonwealth be given a 'concurrent power to legislate with respect to all aspects of corporate activity and the securities industry' (Constitutional Commission, 1987c, p. 5), with concerns about the operation of the finance sector, rather than industrial relations, being the major basis of the recommendation.

If the recommendations of these two committees were incorporated into the Constitution, they would have profound implications for the operation of Australian industrial relations. The power of the Commonwealth government vis-à-vis both the commission and the states would be substantially enhanced. Via section 109 of the Constitution the Commonwealth government would be able to override inconsistent legislation of state governments. Were the Commonwealth government to initiate action to make these recommendations referendum proposals, they would be vigorously opposed by supporters of states' rights.

The *Australian judicial system committee* has offered comments and a recommendation that are relevant to the Hancock Report. While supporting the *Boilermakers* case and the separation-of-powers doctrine, the committee maintains that the Hancock Report's proposals concerning dual appointments to both a commission and a court 'could in our view be implemented consistently with the *Boilermakers* case, and without the need for constitutional amendment' (Constitutional Commission, 1987a, p. 67). In addition, the committee recommended that the Constitution should be amended to enable cross-vesting between Commonwealth and state courts. If this recommendation was acted upon, it would enhance co-operation between Commonwealth and state industrial relations systems and tribunals, such as the Hancock Report had postulated.

CONCLUSION

In May 1987 the Hawke government introduced a legislative package based principally on the 1985 Hancock Report. Employers and business groups vigorously opposed the enforcement and compliance provisions, but were saved thousands of advertising dollars when the Hawke government withdrew the Industrial Relations Bill after deciding to call a snap federal election.

At the end of July 1987 the ACTU and the TDC released *Australia Reconstructed*, which derives from a fact-finding mission to Western Europe. *Australia Reconstructed* constitutes a Swedish-based corporatist blueprint designed to achieve economic growth via the creation of a National Development Fund and the redistribution of resources to the manufacturing- and export-competing sectors. Except in the industry-policy, education, and retraining areas the Hawke government's response has been lukewarm. A major obstacle to acceptance of *Australia Reconstructed* is that it advocates more-corporatist centralization at a time when Australia seems to be groping towards decentralization.

Throughout 1987 a number of reports with industrial relations implications were issued by the Advisory Committee to the Constitutional Commission established in 1985. A substantial increase of Commonwealth powers would be afforded by proposals for direct, Commonwealth industrial relations power and power to manage the national economy (and 'all aspects of corporate activity'). Equally the federalist nature of industrial relations in Australia would be altered if the Constitutional Commission's changes were effected.

NOTES

1 See the *Australian Financial Review*, 13 May 1987.
2 It should be noted that while championing common law rights with respect to industrial disputes, employers had not been so concerned with the common law rights of injured workers when various state workers compensation Acts were changed to impose fixed, or maximum, rates of compensation in an attempt to reduce costs.
3 See the *Australian Financial Review*, 15 May and 25 May 1987, the *Sydney Morning Herald*, 15 and 26 May 1987, and the *Australian*, 19, 23, 26, and 27 May 1987.

4 See the ACTU's *Future Strategies*: 'In the medium to long term the union movement must seriously consider what form of sanctioning regime it is prepared to accept as part of a fair and balanced industrial relations system' (ACTU, 1987, p. 9).

5 The Business Council of Australia sent its own study group to Sweden in October 1986. The study group questioned both the success of the Swedish model and its applicability to Australia (BCA, 1986).

6 For an account of industry policy in Australia see Ewer, Higgins, and Stevens (1987).

CHAPTER 8

A Decade of Continuous Change

The 1980s have been interesting for Australian industrial relations. At the macro level there has been continual change as the systems of wage determination and industrial relations regulation have been adjusted in response to changes in political ideologies and power bases as well as the pressures of economic downturns and changing lobbies. Defining industrial relations reform as a change in procedural rules (see Chapter 4), all of the changes that have been either implemented or proposed constitute examples of industrial relations reform. Australian industrial relations in the 1980s has been awash with reform proposals and has continually experimented with and undergone reform.[1] If nothing else, the 1980s have proved that the Australian system of industrial relations is far from inflexible, unchanging, and rigid.

This study has been concerned with the major reforms that have been implemented and experimented with, the 'successful' reforms, as well as those 'unsuccessful' reforms that have been advocated but, to date, have not been implemented or adopted. Table 8.1 summarizes the six major 'successful' reforms of the 1980s and indicates the major parties' support for or opposition to these reforms.

The decade began with industrial relations being regulated by a centralized system based on wage indexation which the Australian Conciliation and Arbitration Commission had introduced and operated in response to Australia's economic and industrial relations problems dating from the mid-1970s. In both the second half of the 1970s and the early 1980s, wage indexation was advocated by the commission and supported by the Australian Council of Trade Unions (ACTU) and opposed by the Fraser Liberal—National Party government and the Confederation of Australian Industry (CAI).

In the early 1980s Australia experienced economic growth, associated with what turned out to be a short-lived mining and resources boom. In this more favourable economic environment, parties in both the private and the public sectors reached agreements which clearly breached the commission's wage indexation guidelines. In response to this the commission brought wage indexation to an end in July 1981 and ushered in a decentralized system of industrial relations regulation. With the exception of the commission, which wished to continue to operate a centralized system based on wage indexation, all of the major parties supported this move to decentralization.

The second half of 1982 witnessed a substantial deterioration in the Australian economy, with marked increases in both the level of inflation and unemployment (both in the order of 10 per cent). Many commentators believed that Australia was experiencing its worst economic crisis since the Depression of the 1930s. Following an application by the Fraser coalition government, which was supported by both the CAI and the ACTU, the commission introduced a wages freeze in December 1982. Among other things, the wages freeze returned Australia to a centralized system of industrial relations regulation.

Under the leadership of former ACTU president Bob Hawke the Australian Labor Party (ALP) won the March 1983 federal election. Prior to the election the Hawke-led ALP entered into the Accord (Mark I) with the ACTU, involving both in a series of undertakings and a policy program which would be pursued by the ALP if it won office. A major feature of the Accord Mark I was a commitment to the maintenance of real wages over time. The election of the Hawke Labor government heralded a return to a centralized system based on wage indexation, a system that had been experimented with, and abandoned, between April 1975 and July 1981.

During the election campaign Hawke pledged that if the ALP won the election, he would hold a National Economic Summit Conference, bringing governments, employers, unions, and other interest groups together in an attempt to devise a program of national reconciliation based on co-operation and consensus and implementation of an incomes policy. While the CAI was one of the many employer/business groups that attended and endorsed the communiqué which resulted from the summit, it had not been included in the drawing up of the Accord and opposed the commission's reintroduction of wage indexation in September 1983.

In 1985 Australia began to experience major balance of payments problems, with substantial falls in the terms of trade and the value of the Australian dollar, and increases in the level of external debt. In response to these problems the Hawke government and the ACTU, in September 1985, negotiated the Accord Mark II, which recognized the need to discount wage-indexation-based national wage case increases for the price effects associated with the depreciation of the Australian dollar. As with the Accord Mark I, the CAI was not included in the drawing up of the Accord Mark II and opposed its introduction before the commission.

As Australia's international economic problems continued into 1986 and 1987 all of the major parties came to the realization that wage indexation was no longer sustainable. In March 1987, with the support of the parties, the commission introduced a two-tiered system that combined elements of centralization and decentralization. While still allowing a role for national wage cases, albeit a lesser role, the two-tiered system was an attempt to link wage increases to microeconomic efficiency and restructuring (or productivity).

Following the planned expiry of the two-tiered system Australia will develop a new system of wage determination and industrial relations regulation — its seventh for the decade. It will be interesting to observe if the momentum for decentralization and the linkage of wage rises to microeconomic efficiency (or productivity), established by the two-tiered system, will be maintained. Employers may be expected to support a productivity-based system of wage determination. The Hawke government, given its concern to alleviate Australia's international economic problems, may also be expected to support such a system. If the Hawke government adopts this stance, strain would undoubtedly

Table 8.1   Major Forms of Wage Determination and Industrial Relations Regulation, and Attitudes of Major Parties in the 1980s

System and Period	Commonwealth Government	Commission	CAI	ACTU
1 Wage Indexation January 1980–July 1981	0	+	0	+
2 Decentralization July 1981–December 1982	+	0	+	+
3 Wages Freeze December 1982–September 1983	+	+	+	+
4 Accord (Mark I) September 1983–September 1985	+	+	0	+
5 Accord (Mark II) September 1985–March 1987	+	+	0	+
6 Two-tiered System March 1987–?	+	+	+	+

+ support; 0 opposition

be placed on what remains of the Accord, and there would be strong resistance from the ACTU and its affiliates. In the event of economic recovery the ACTU may be expected to support a return to a centralized system with wage rises linked to movements in prices.

The apparently variable and fluid nature of the cartels involved in and with these 'successful' reforms (see Table 8.1) is noteworthy. There have been only two occasions when all major parties concurred — the Fraser government's wages freeze, and the introduction of the two-tiered system. Only the ACTU has supported all of the reforms. Since this may be attributed to pragmatism and a desire to influence events from the 'inside', ACTU concurrence in the event of a Liberal—National Party government winning office, especially if it sought to implement an industrial relations agenda based on the ideas of the New Right, seems less likely. The CAI opposed wage indexation at the beginning of the decade, as well as the Accords. The CAI, with the exception of the wages freeze, has been opposed to centralized systems and has only been prepared to support systems which eschewed wage indexation and linked wages to movements in productivity. Constitutional protection enabled the commission to operate a system of wage indexation in the face of Fraser government and CAI objections. The commission's move towards a decentralised system during the mining and resources boom of the early 1980s had more to do with expediency than a change of heart (see Chapters 2, 5).

The major 'unsuccessful' reforms of the 1980s include the recommendations of the Hancock Report (see Chapter 4), the National Taxation Summit premises (see Chapter 5), and the Industrial Relations Bill, as introduced in 1987 (see Chapter 7). General foment that may be directly attributed to Australia's economic deterioration throughout the 1980s and especially during the second half of the decade has produced reform propositions of varying shades: Chapter 6 details the New Right's internecine warfare against unions and industrial tribunals, and Chapter 7 discusses the ACTU—Trade Development Council proposal for a National Development Fund, as part of a Swedish-style corporatist solution to Australia's economic and industrial

relations woes, as well as amendments to the Australian Constitution that would have far-reaching implications for the operation
of the country's industrial relations systems and regulations.

Throughout, 'How corporatist is Australia?' is the question
that is begged or addressed. At one level, wage indexation, the
so-called consensus policies of the Hawke government, and the
development and application of centralized systems of industrial
relations regulation all have the appearance of being consistent
with corporatism. However, a number of problems can be
identified in applying the corporatist tag to Australia.

Translation of the theoretical insights of corporatism into
useful empirical constructs is difficult. Chapters 1 and 3 query
the usefulness of describing social systems as partially or less
than fully corporatist and discuss the conceptual problems inherent in applying real-world corporatist parts to a real-world
pluralist whole. The National Taxation Summit, convened in
July 1985, when the Hawke government was still maintaining its
consensus and corporatist orientation, was in fact consistent
with a (societal) pluralist approach. Equally, employers and
business organizations have been racked by conflict and dissension
as they have attempted to negotiate a way for themselves across
the shifting ground that corporatist—pluralist unions, governments, and industrial tribunals must represent.

Australian industrial relations in the 1980s has been too
flexible and adaptable to permit it to be viewed merely as
antipodean corporatism. Corporatist theory does not explain
Australian industrial relations' facility in switching between
centralization and decentralization or its ability to cope with the
major parties' frequent changes in cartels during the 1980s.

The theory of episodic equilibria[2], based above all on the
inevitability of change, is offered as an alternative to corporatist
theory. The equilibria are the 'successful' reform proposals of
the 1980s, summarized in Table 8.1. These 'successful' reforms
are viewed as a stream of equilibrium points. Given the environment which pervades industrial relations at a given point in
time the groups and organizations involved in industrial relations
compete, come into conflict and struggle with each other in
seeking to achieve the realization of their respective goals. A

particular power base — perhaps equilibrium — will always be established. This (and other) fulcrums establish a particular 'reform', that is, a set of procedural rules. The establishment of an equilibrium point does not of course mean that there is an end to competition, conflict, or the authority struggle.

Change is episodic, its timing and particular form difficult if not impossible to predict.[3] The establishment of equilibria, and/or the movement from one point of equilibrium to another, result from the *interaction* of exogenous and endogenous variables. The major exogenous (external) variable which this study has considered is the macroeconomic performance of the Australian economy; changes in the Australian economy have been associated with changes in the industrial relations system. It has been demonstrated that economic adversity has been used to justify both the introduction of wage indexation in 1975 and 1983 and the abandoning wage of indexation in 1986. In addition, the development of decentralized systems of industrial relations regulation have been associated with an economy on the upswing, such as the mining and resources boom of 1980 and 1981, and an economy plagued by major balance of payments problems (the two-tiered system was introduced in 1987).

While changes in the macroeconomic performance of an economy create pressures for reform, the reform that will in fact be implemented is never clear. Exogenous pressures for change can be resisted, modified, or overcome by subject groups or 'clubs' (see Chapter 6); an *a priori* negatively or adversely affected group or organisation may be strong enough to resist pressures and may even improve its relative position. For example, it might have been expected at the end of 1982 and the beginning of 1983 that 'Australia's worst economic crisis since the Depression of the 1930s' would make it difficult for unions to win improved concessions for members; in December 1982 the Fraser government established a wages freeze. However, by the end of 1983, wages were once more linked to prices (see Chapter 3).

Endogenous (internal) change results or is derived from the competition, conflict, or authority struggle as those involved in industrial relations interact and seek to achieve their respective organizational goals and objectives. However, the mere desire of a group or organization to achieve reform, or the establishment of a new equilibrium, does not mean that reform will in fact take place. As this study has demonstrated, many reform proposals will fall by the wayside, or be 'unsuccessful'. As with exogenous change, forces for endogenous change can be resisted by those who are opposed to change. Those who desire reform have to be powerful or strong enough to persuade or coerce the groups and organizations they interact with, if they are to succeed in establishing procedural change.

The quantity or quality of reform which does or does not occur will not, therefore, provide any indication, or measure, of the degree of competition, conflict, or struggle that exists between and within the numerous and various groups involved in industrial relations. Movement from one point of equilibrium to another may entail limited conflict or struggle, only because opposing groups did not mobilize quickly enough; remaining at a particular point of equilibrium may be attributable to a high degree of conflict and struggle, or to a lack of awareness of the inevitability of change, or to ignorance of the existence of a (new) adversary; and so on.

The 1980s in Australia have witnessed the establishment of six major forms of industrial relations regulation, or equilibria, with a seventh to commence in the second half of 1988. The decade has also witnessed the floating of a variety of reform proposals which, to date, have not been adopted or implemented. The number and variety of both 'successful' and 'unsuccessful' reforms that have occurred in the 1980s may be considered as extrapolations from the beleaguered Australian economy. Further changes in industrial relations systems and regulations may therefore be expected in the not-too-distant future.

If the Hawke Labor government should adopt a more decentralized (or deregulatory) industrial relations stance in seeking to resolve Australia's international and balance of payments problems, a negative reaction from the ACTU and its affiliates, threatening what is left of the Accord, is virtually inevitable. The election of a Liberal–National Party coalition government would, in all probability, usher in a more deregulated and decentralized industrial relations system, circumscribing and reducing the power of unions. The commission, under the leadership of Mr Justice Maddern, may develop a new approach to industrial relations regulation to take Australia into the 1990s. Unions, employers, and government, and their respective representatives, are already allocating considerable resources to development of new and revised approaches to industrial relations. As ever, there is nothing so inevitable as change.

NOTES

1 In saying this it should be realised that this study has focused on major macro-level changes. It has not considered developments at the state level and the reforms initiated and suggested in the areas of equal employment opportunity, occupational health and safety, and industrial democracy.
2 Episodic equilibria is different from punctuated equilibria as developed by Eldredge and Gould in their attempt to unravel the mysteries of evolution and natural history. See Gould (1983, pp. 149–54).
3 There are two things we can say with certainty about the future: first, we do not know what the future holds; second, we know that we do not know what the future holds.

Bibliography

Accord (1983) (1985). *See* Statement of Accord *and* Agreement Between the Government and the ACTU.

ACPI, *see* Advisory Committee on Prices.

ACTU, *see* Australian Council of Trade Unions.

Addison, J. T. (1984), 'Trade Unions, Corporatism, and Inflation', *Journal of Labor Research*, Winter.

Advisory Committee on Prices and Incomes (ACPI), Department of Industrial Relations (1987), *Price Surveillance in Australia*, AGPS, Canberra.

Advisory Committee to the Constitutional Commission (1987a), *Australian Judicial System*, AGPS, Canberra

Advisory Committee to the Constitutional Commission (1987b), *Distribution of Powers*, AGPS, Canberra.

Advisory Committee to the Constitutional Commission (1987c), *Trade and National Economic Management*, AGPS, Canberra.

Agreement Between the Government and the ACTU for the Discounting of Wages Indexation and Ongoing Wage Restraint (1985), 4 September, mimeo. (Accord Mark II).

Allen, V. L. (1971), *The Sociology of Industrial Relations*, Longman, London.

Anderson, C. W. (1977), 'Political Design and the Representation of Interests', *Comparative Political Studies*, April.

Arbitration in Contempt (1986), H. R. Nicholls Society, Melbourne.

Attorney-General, Department of (1986), *Dispute Resolution in Commercial Matters: Papers* (Colloquium, Australian Academy of Science), AGPS, Canberra.

Australian Bureau of Statistics, *Industrial Disputes*, Cat. Nos 6321.0 and 6322.0, *The Labour Force — Australia*, Cat. No. 6203.0, *Labour Reports*, Ref. No. 6.6, *Wage Rate Indexes (Preliminary)*, Cat. No. 6311.0.

Australian Constitution.

Australian Council of Trade Unions (ACTU) (1987), *Future Strategies for the Trade Union Movement*.

Australian Law Journal Review.

Australian Law Reports.

Australia Reconstructed, see Department of Trade.

Baldwin, J. R. (1975), *The Regulatory Agency and the Public Corporation: the Canadian Air Transport Industry*, Ballinger, Cambridge, Mass.

Barkin, D. (1971), *American Pluralist Democracy: a Critique*, Van Nostrand Reinhold Company, New York.

BCA, *see* Business Council of Australia.

Bernstein, M. H. (1955), *Regulating Business by Independent Commission*, Princeton University Press, Princeton.

Blackburn, M. (1940), 'Trade Unionism: Its Operation Under Australian Law', Victorian Labor College, Melbourne.

Blandy, R. and Niland, J., editors (1986), *Alternatives to Arbitration*, Allen and Unwin, Sydney.

Boehm, E. A. (1974), 'Distortions in Relative Wages: the Inflationary Consequences and Policy Implications', *Australian Economic Review*, No. 4.

Booth, A. (1982), 'Corporatism, Capitalism and Depression in Twentieth-Century Britain', *British Journal of Sociology*, June.

Bray, M. and Taylor, V., editors (1986), *Managing Labour? Essays in the Political Economy of Australian Industrial Relations*, McGraw-Hill, Sydney.

Bruno, M. and Sachs, J. (1985), *Economics of Worldwide Stagflation*, Basil Blackwell, Oxford.

Business Council of Australia (BCA) (1986), 'Industrial Relations In Sweden: Report of Business Council of Australia Study Mission to Sweden, October 1986', *Business Council Bulletin*, October.

CAI, *see* Confederation of Australian Industry.

Canadian Report, *see* Task Force on Labour Relations.

Clegg, H. A. (1975), 'Pluralism in Industrial Relations', *British Journal of Industrial Relations*, November.

Coghill, K., editor (1987), *The New Right's Australian Fantasy*, McPhee Gribble, Fitzroy.

Colebatch, H. K. (1986), 'Organisation and Political Analysis', *Politics*, May.

Collins, J. (1978), 'Fragmentation of the Working Class', in E. L. Wheelwright and K. Buckley, editors, *Essays in the Political Economy of Australian Capitalism*, Volume 3, Australia and New Zealand Book Co., Sydney.

Committee of Inquiry on Co-ordinated Industrial Organisations (1974), *Report*, AGPS, Canberra. (Sweeney Report).

Committee of Review of Australian Industrial Relations Law and Systems (1985), *Report*, 3 volumes, AGPS, Canberra. (Hancock Report).

Commonwealth Arbitration Reports.

Commonwealth Law Reports.

Confederation of Australian Industry (CAI) (1986), 'Industrial Fantasies', *Industrial Review*, November.

Confederation of Australian Industry (CAI) (1987), *Employer Perspectives on the ACTU/TDC Report 'Australia Reconstructed'*, Melbourne.

Connolly, W. E., editor (1969), *The Bias of Pluralism*, Atherton Press, New York.

Constitutional Commission, *see* Advisory Committee to the Constitutional Commission.

Costello, P. (1986), 'The Trade Union Reform Act of 1987', *IPA Review*, Spring.

Crawford, B. and Volard, S. (1981), 'Work Absence in Industrialised Societies: the Australian Case', *Industrial Relations Journal*, May–June.

Creighton, W. B., Ford, W. J., and Mitchell, R. J. (1983), *Labour Law: Materials and Commentary*, Law Book Co., Sydney.

Crouch, C. (1977), *Class Conflict and the Industrial Relations Crisis: Compromise and Corporatism in the Policies of the British State*, Humanities Press, London.

Crouch, C. (1979a), *The Politics of Industrial Relations*, Fontana/Collins, Glasgow.

Crouch, C., editor (1979b), *State and Economy in Contemporary Capitalism*, Croom Helm, London.

Crouch, C. (1982), *Trade Unions: The Logic of Collective Action*, Fontana, Glasgow.

Cupper, L. (1976), 'Legalism in the Australian Conciliation and Arbitration Commission: the Gradual Transition', *Journal of Industrial Relations*, December.

d'Alpuget, B. (1982), *Robert J. Hawke: a Biography*, Schwartz, East Melbourne.

Dabscheck, B. (1977), 'The Internal Authority of the ACTU', *Journal of Industrial Relations*, December.

Dabscheck, B. (1980), 'The Australian System of Industrial Relations: An Analytical Model', *Journal of Industrial Relations*, June.

Dabscheck, B. (1983), *Arbitrator at Work: Sir William Raymond Kelly and the Regulation of Australian Industrial Relations*, George Allen and Unwin, Sydney.

Dabscheck, B. (1984), 'Menzies's Unforgettable 1951 National Economic Summit', *Journal of Industrial Relations*, September.

Dabscheck, B. (1986), 'Tribunals and Wage Determination: the Problem of Co-ordination' in J. Niland, editor, *Wage Fixation in Australia*, Allen and Unwin, Sydney.

Dabscheck, B. and Niland, J. (1981), *Industrial Relations in Australia*, George Allen and Unwin, Sydney.

Dahrendorf, R. (1959), *Class and Class Conflict in an Industrial Society*, Routledge and Kegan Paul, London.

Davis, K. (1985), 'The Queensland Power Dispute: An Industrial Watershed?', *Quadrant*, June.

DEIR, *see* Department of Employment and Industrial Relations.

Department of Employment and Industrial Relations (DEIR) (1985), *Review of Australian Law and Practice in Relation to Conventions Adopted by the International Labour Conference*, AGPS, Canberra.

Department of Trade (1987), *Australia Reconstructed — ACTU/TDC*

Mission to Western Europe: a Report by the Mission Members to the ACTU and the TDC, AGPS, Canberra.

Donovan Report, *see* Royal Commission on Trade Unions and Employers Associations.

Draft White Paper, *see Reform of the Australian Tax System*.

Dunlop, J. T. (1958), *Industrial Relations Systems*, Holt, New York.

Ehrlick, S. and Wooton, G., editors (1980), *Three Faces of Pluralism: Political, Ethnic and Religious*, Gower, Westmead.

Eldridge, J. E. T. (1971), *Sociology and Industrial Life*, Nelson, London.

Ewer, P., Higgins, W., and Stevens, A. (1987), *Unions and the Future of Australian Manufacturing*, Allen and Unwin, Sydney.

Federal Law Review.

Flanders, A. (1965), *Industrial Relations: What is Wrong With the System*, Faber and Faber and Institute of Personnel Management, London.

Fox, A. (1966), *Industrial Sociology and Industrial Relations*, Research Paper 3, Royal Commission on Trade Unions and Employers' Associations, HMSO, London.

Fox, A. (1973), 'Industrial Relations: a Social Critique of Pluralist Ideology', in J. Child, editor, *Man and Organization: the Search for Explanation and Social Relevance*, George Allen and Unwin, London.

Fox, A. (1974), *Beyond Contract: Work, Power and Trust Relations*, Faber and Faber, London.

Fox, A. (1979), 'A Note on Industrial Relations Pluralism', *Sociology*, January.

Fox, A. and Flanders, A. (1969), 'The Reform of Collective Bargaining: from Donovan to Durkheim', *British Journal of Industrial Relations*, June.

Fuerstenberg, F. (1987), 'The Federal Republic of Germany', in G. J. Bamber and R. D. Lansbury, editors, *International and Comparative Industrial Relations*, Allen and Unwin, Sydney.

Future Strategies, see Australian Council of Trade Unions.

Gerritsen, R. (1986), 'The Necessity of "Corporatism": the Case of the Hawke Labor Government', *Politics*, May.

Gill, F. (1985), 'Over-Award Payments; Results of a Survey Conducted in 1982', Working Papers in Economics No. 85, Department of Economics, University of Sydney, December.

Goldberg, V. P. (1976), 'Regulation and Administered Contracts', *Bell Journal of Economics*, Autumn.

Goldthorpe, J. H. (1969), 'Social Inequality and Social Integration in Modern Britain', *Advancement of Science*, December.

Goldthorpe, J. H. (1977), 'Industrial Relations in Great Britain: A Critique of Reformism', in T. Clarke and L. Clements, editors, *Trade Unions Under Capitalism*, Fontana/Collins, Glasgow.

Gould, S. J. (1983), *The Panda's Thumb: More Reflections in Natural History*, Penguin, Harmondsworth.

Groenewegen, P. D. (1985), 'The National Taxation Summit: Success or Failure? An Overview of the Major Issues', *Economic Papers*, September.

Gruen, F. H. (1983), 'The Prices and Incomes Accord, Employment, and Unemployment', *Economic Papers*, October.

Guille, H. (1985), 'Industrial Relations in Queensland', *Journal of Industrial Relations*, September.

Gutman, G. D. (1986), 'Australian Industrial Relations: Revamping the System. A Bicentenary Offering', *Quadrant*, April.

Hagan, J. (1981), *The History of the ACTU*, Longman Cheshire, Melbourne.

Hammarstrom, O. (1987), 'Sweden', in G. J. Bamber and R. D. Lansbury, editors, *International and Comparative Industrial Relations*, Allen and Unwin, Sydney.

Hancock Report *see* Committee of Review of Australian Industrial Relations Law and Systems.

Henderson, G. (1983), 'The Industrial Relations Club', *Quadrant*, September.

Higgins, H. B. (1915), 'A New Province for Law and Order', *Harvard Law Review*, November.

High Court Decisions.

Howard, W. A. (1977), 'Australian Trade Unions in the Context of Union Theory', *Journal of Industrial Relations*, September.

Hurst, J. (1983), *Hawke PM*, Angus and Robertson, Sydney.

Hyde, J. and Nurick, J., editors (1985), *Wages Wasteland: the Australian Wage Fixing System*, Hale and Iremonger and Australian Institute for Public Policy, Sydney.

Hyman, R. (1971), *Marxism and the Sociology of Trade Unions*, Pluto, London.

Hyman, R. (1975), *Industrial Relations: a Marxist Introduction*, Macmillan, London.

Hyman, R. (1978), 'Pluralism, Procedural Consensus and Collective Bargaining', *British Journal of Industrial Relations*, March.

Hyman, R. (1980), 'Theory in Industrial Relations: Towards a Materialist Analysis', in P. Boreham and G. Dow, editors, *Work and Inequality: Ideology and Control in the Capitalist Labour Process*, Volume 2, Macmillan, South Melbourne.

Hyman, R. and Brough, I. (1975), *Social Values and Industrial Relations: a Study of Fairness and Inequality*, Blackwell, Oxford.

Hyman, R. and Fryer, B. (1975), 'Trade Unions — Sociology and Political Economy', in J. B. McKinlay, editor, *Processing People: Cases in Organisational Behaviour*, Holt, Rinehart and Winston, London.

Industrial Relations Bill (1987).

Isaac, J. E. (1977), 'Wage Determination and Economic Policy', *Australian Economic Review*, No. 3.

Isaac, J. E. (1982), 'Economics and Industrial Relations', *Journal of Industrial Relations*, December.

Isaac, J. E. (1986), 'The Meaning and Significance of Comparative

Wage Justice', in J. Niland, editor, *Wage Fixation in Australia*, Allen and Unwin, Sydney.

Jacobi, O. (1985), 'World Economic Changes and Industrial Relations in the Federal Republic of Germany', in H. Juris, M. Thompson, and W. Daniels, editors, *Industrial Relations in a Decade of Economic Change*, Industrial Relations Research Association, Madison.

Jenkins, L. (1986), The Rise and Fall of Superannuation in Australian Industrial Relations, Bachelor of Commerce (Industrial Relations) Honours thesis, University of New South Wales.

Jessop, B. (1977), 'Recent Theories of the Capitalist State', *Cambridge Journal of Economics*, December.

Joskow, P.L. (1974), 'Inflation and Environmental Concern: Structural Change in the Process of Public Utility Price Regulation', *Journal of Law and Economics*, October.

Kelly, P. (1984), *The Hawke Ascendancy: a Definitive Account of its Origins and Climax 1975−1983*, Angus and Robertson, Sydney.

Kelso, W. A. (1978), *American Democratic Theory: Pluralism and its Critics*, Greenwood Press, Westport.

Kemp, D. A. (1983), 'The National Economic Summit: Authority, Persuasion and Exchange', *The Economic Record*, September.

Kerr, C. (1964), *Labour and Management in Industrial Society*, Anchor Books Doubleday, New York.

Kerr, C. *et al.* (1973), *Industrialism and Industrial Man*, Penguin, Ringwood.

Kochan, T. A. (1980), *Collective Bargaining and Industrial Relations: from Theory to Policy and Practice*, Richard D. Irwin, Homewood.

Kochan, T. A., McKersie, R. B., and Cappelli, P. (1984), 'Strategic Choice and Industrial Relations Theory', *Industrial Relations*, Winter.

Kriesi, H. (1982), 'The Structure of the Swiss Political System' in G. Lehmbruch, and P. C. Schmitter, editors, *Patterns of Corporatist Policy-Making*, Sage, London.

Kyloh, R. (1985), *Overaward Payments and Wage Flexibility*, Wages and Incomes Policy Research Paper No. 5., Department of Employment and Industrial Relations, Canberra.

Lash, S. (1985), 'The End of Neo-Corporatism?: the Breakdown of Centralised Bargaining in Sweden', *British Journal of Industrial Relations*, July.

Leard, J. (1986), *Australia. The worst is yet to come*, John Leard, Parramatta.

Lee, M. (1980), The Industrial Peace Act 1920: a Study of Political Interference in Compulsory Arbitration, Master of Economics thesis, University of Sydney.

Lehmbruch, G. (1977), 'Liberal Corporatism and Party Government', *Comparative Political Studies*, April.

Lenin, V. I. (1970), 'What Is To Be Done?', in *Lenin on Trade Unions*, Progress Publishers, Moscow.

Loveday, P. (1984), 'Corporatist Trends in Australia', *Politics*, May.

Ludeke, J. T. (1986), 'The Voluntary System of Conciliation and Arbitration: a Role for the Tribunals', in R. Blandy and J. Niland, editors, *Alternatives to Arbitration*, Allen and Unwin, Sydney.

McCallum, R. C. (1984), 'Federal Controls Upon Trade Unions: the Australian Enigma', in D. Rawson and C. Fisher, editors, *Changing Industrial Law*, Croom Helm, Sydney.

McCarthy, P. (1985), 'Power Without Glory: the Queensland Electricity Dispute', *Journal of Industrial Relations*, September.

McEachern, D. (1985), 'National Economic Summit: Business and the Hawke Government', *Journal of Australian Political Economy*, December.

McEachern, D. (1986), 'Corporatism and Business Responses to the Hawke Government', *Politics*, May.

McFarland, A. S. (1969), *Power and Leadership in Pluralist Systems*, Stanford University Press, Stanford.

McGuinness, P. P. (1985), *The Case Against the Arbitration Commission*, Centre for Independent Studies, Sydney.

Maddern, J. (1986), Statement by the President, 8 July, mimeo.

Margerison, C. J. (1969), 'What Do We Mean by Industrial Relations? A Behavioural Science Approach', *British Journal of Industrial Relations*, July.

Markovits, A. S. and Allen, C. S. (1984), 'Trade Unions and the Economic Crisis: the West German Case', in P. Gourevitch *et al.*, *Unions and Economic Crisis: Britain, West Germany, and Sweden*, George Allen and Unwin, London.

Martin, A. (1984), 'Trade Unions in Sweden: Strategic Responses to Change and Crisis', in P. Gourevitch *et al.*, *Unions and Economic Crisis: Britain, West Germany, and Sweden*, George Allen and Unwin, London.

Martin, R. M. (1958), 'The rise of the Australian Council of Trade Unions', *The Australian Quarterly*, March.

Martin, R. (1980), *Trade Unionism in Australia*, Penguin, Ringwood.

Martin, R. M. (1983), 'Pluralism and the New Corporatism', *Political Studies*, March.

Miliband, R. (1973), *The State in Capitalist Society: the Analysis of the Western System of Power*, Quartet, London.

Mitchell, R. (1986), The Trend to Evasion of the Arbitral System of Industrial Dispute Settlement: Recent Developments in the Australian Federal Jurisdiction, Working Paper, Labour Studies Programme, Faculty of Economics and Commerce, University of Melbourne, September.

Mitchell, R. J. (1976), 'Liability in Tort for Causing Economic Loss by the Use of Unlawful Means and its Application to Australian Industrial Disputes', *Adelaide Law Review*, November.

Mulvey, C. (1983), 'Wages Policy and Wage Determination in 1982', *Journal of Industrial Relations*, March.

Mulvey, C. (1984), 'Wages Policy and Wage Determination in 1983', *Journal of Industrial Relations*, March.

Mulvey, C. (1985), 'Wages Policy and Wage Determination in 1984', *Journal of Industrial Relations*, March.

Murray, R. (1970), *The Split: Australian Labor in the Fifties*, Cheshire, Melbourne.

Nairn, B. (1973), *Civilising Capitalism: the Labour Movement in New South Wales 1870–1900*, Australian National University Press, Canberra.

National Economic Summit Conference Documents and Proceedings (1983), Vol. 2, *Record of Proceedings*, AGPS, Canberra.

National Taxation Summit: Record of Proceedings (1985), AGPS, Canberra.

National Wage Cases (NWC).

Nicholls, D. (1974), *Three Varieties of Pluralism*, Macmillan, London.

NWC (National Wage Cases).

Ormonde, P. (1972), *The Movement*, Nelson, Melbourne.

Panitch, L. (1977), 'The Development of Corporatism in Liberal Democracies', *Comparative Political Studies*, April.

Panitch, L. (1980), 'Recent Theorization of Corporatism: Reflections on a Growth Industry', *British Journal of Sociology*, June.

Panitch, L. (1981), 'Trade Unions and the Capitalist State', *New Left Review*, January–February.

Peetz, D. (1985), *A Descriptive Examination of Superannuation Coverage by Industry and Occupation*, Wages and Incomes Policy Division, Department of Employment and Industrial Relations.

Pemberton, J. and Davis, G. (1986), 'The Rhetoric of Consensus', *Politics*, May.

Perlman, S. (1949), *A Theory of the Labour Movement*, Augustus and Kelley, New York.

Peterson, R. B. (1985), 'Economic and Political Impacts on the Swedish Model of Industrial Relations', in H. Juris, M. Thompson, and W. Daniels, editors, *Industrial Relations in a Decade of Economic Change*, Industrial Relations Research Association, Madison.

Plowman, D. H. (1981), *Wage Indexation: a Study of Australian Wage Issues, 1975–80*, George Allen and Unwin, Sydney.

Porter, M. E. and Sagansky, J. F. (1976), 'Information Politics and Economic Analysis: the Regulatory Decision Process in Air Freight Cases', *Public Policy*, Spring.

Posner, A. (1974), 'Theories of Economic Regulation', *Bell Journal of Economics and Management Science*, Autumn.

Provis, C. (1986), 'Comparative Wage Justice', *Journal of Industrial Relations*, March.

Rawson, D. W. and Wrightson, S. (1985), *Australian Unions 1984*, Croom Helm, Sydney.

Reform of the Australian Tax System (1985), Draft White Paper, AGPS, Canberra.

Report of Consultants to Department of Industrial Relations on the (Commonwealth) *Conciliation and Arbitration Act 1904* (1981), October, mimeo. (Searby and Taylor Report.)

Richardson, S. (1982), 'The Skilled Metal Trades', in R. Blandy and S. Richardson, editors, *How Labour Markets Work: Case Studies in Adjustment*, Longman Cheshire, Melbourne.

Rickard, J. (1984), *H. B. Higgins: the Rebel as Judge*, George Allen and Unwin, Sydney.

Roe, M. (1984), *Nine Australian Progressives: Vitalism in Bourgeois Social Thought 1890–1960*, University of Queensland Press, St Lucia.

Romeyn, J. (1980), 'Towards a Motivational Theory of Arbitration in Australia', *Journal of Industrial Relations*, June.

Royal Commission on Trade Unions and Employers Associations (1965–68), *Report*, HMSO, London. (Donovan Report.)

Sawer, M., editor (1982), *Australia and The New Right*, George Allen and Unwin, Sydney.

Schmitter, P. C. (1974), 'Still the Century of Corporatism', in P. C. Schmitter and G. Lehmbruch, editors, *Trends Towards Corporatist Intermediation*, Sage Publications, Beverly Hills.

Schott, K. (1984), *Policy, Power and Order: the Persistence of Economic Problems in Capitalist States*, Yale University Press, New Haven.

Schott, K. (1985), 'The Consensus Economy: an International Overview', *Economic Papers*, June.

Searby and Taylor Report, *see* Report of Consultants.

Shaw, J. W. and Harris, G. P. (1986), 'Who Was H. R. Nicholls?', *Industrial Relations Society of New South Wales Newsletter*, September.

Sheridan, T. (1973), 'Labour v Labor: The Victorian Metal Trades Dispute of 1946–47', in J. Iremonger, J. Merritt and Graeme Osborne, editors, *Strikes: Studies in Twentieth Century Australian Social History*, Angus and Robertson, Sydney.

Sheridan, T. (1975), *Mindful Militants: the Amalgamated Engineering Union in Australia 1920–72*, Cambridge University Press, Cambridge.

Sheridan, T. (1986), Planners and the Australian Labour Market 1945–1949, Working Paper, Department of Economics, University of Adelaide.

Singleton, G. (1985), 'The Economic Planning Advisory Council: the Reality of Consensus', *Politics*, May.

South Australian Industrial Reports.

Statement of Accord By the Australian Labor Party and the Australian Council of Trade Unions Regarding Economic Policy (1983), mimeo. (Accord Mark I.)

Steinke, J. (1983), 'The Long-term Decline in the Standard Working Year', *Journal of Industrial Relations*, December.

Stepan, A. (1978), *The State and Society: Peru in Comparative Perspective*, Princeton University Press, Princeton.

Stewart, R. G. (1985), 'The Politics of the Accord: Does Corporatism Explain It?', *Politics*, May.

Stewart, R. and Ballard, J. (1985), 'A Funny Thing Happened on the Way to the Tax Summit — Hawke Discovered the Limits to Corporatism', in D. Jaenesch and N. Bierbaum, editors, *Proceedings of 27th Annual Conference, APSA, Adelaide*, Volume 2, *The Hawke Government — Past, Present, Future*.

Stigler, G. J. (1971), 'The Theory of Economic Regulation', *Bell Journal of Economic And Management Science*, Spring.

Stilwell, F. (1986), *The Accord and Beyond: the Political Economy of the Labor Government*, Pluto Press, Sydney.

Stone, J. O. (1984a), '1929 and All That', *Australian Economic Review*, 3rd Quarter.

Stone, J. (1984b), 'What Kind of Country? In the Decade Ahead and Beyond', *Quadrant*, December.

Stone, J. O. (1985a), 'The Scandal of the Young Unemployed', *Quadrant*, August.

Stone, J. (1985b), 'Deregulate or Perish. Signs of a Society in Decay', *Quadrant*, October.

Stone, J. (1986), 'National Issues', *IPA Review*, Spring.

Stremski, R. (1986), *Kill for Collingwood*, Allen and Unwin, Sydney.

Strinati, D. (1982), *Capitalism, the State and Industrial Relations*, Croom Helm, London.

Summit, *see National Economic Summit Conference.*

Sweeney Report, *see Committee of Inquiry.*

Tarantelli, E. (1986), 'The Regulation of Inflation and Unemployment', *Industrial Relations*, Winter.

Task Force on Labour Relations (1968), *Canadian Industrial Relations*, Queen's Printer, Ottawa. (Canadian Report.)

Taxation Summit, *see National Taxation Summit.*

Taylor, V. (1982), Australian Industrial Relations Research and the Need for Heretics, paper presented at 52nd ANZAAS Congress, Macquarie University, 10–14 May, mimeo.

Thompson, V., Brandis, G., and Harley, T., editors (1986), *Australian Liberalism: the Continuing Vision*, Liberal Forum, Melbourne.

Thurow, L. C. (1983), *Dangerous Currents: the State of Economics*, Oxford University Press, Oxford.

Transport Workers Award, 1 September 1981 (No. 1440, 1981).

von Beyme, K. (1980), *Challenge to Power: Trade Unions and Industrial Relations in Capitalist Countries*, Sage Publications, Beverly Hills.

West, K. (1984), *The Revolution in Australian Politics*, Penguin, Ringwood.

Williams, P. (1986a), 'Union Busters: Their Tactics and Targets', *Business Review Weekly*, 22 August.

Williams, P. (1986b), 'Liberals' Secret Plan to Crack Union Power', *Business Review Weekly*, 5 December.

Willis, R. (1987), Second Reading Speech, 14 May, mimeo.

Wilson, J. Q. (1971), 'The Dead Hand of Regulation', *Public Interest*, Fall.

Wilson, J. Q. (1974), 'The Politics of Regulation', in J. W. Makie, editor, *Social Responsibility and the Business Predicament*, Brookings Institution, Washington, DC.

Wilson, J. Q. (1978), *The Investigators: Managing FBI and Narcotics Agents*, Basic Books, New York.

Wilson, J. Q., editor (1980), *The Politics of Regulation*, Basic Books, New York.

Winkler, J. T. (1976), 'Corporatism', *European Journal of Sociology*, January.

Wolff, R. P. (1969), 'Beyond Tolerance', in R. P. Wolff, B. Moore, and H. Marcuse, *A Critique of Pure Tolerance*, Jonathon Cape, London.

Wood, S. and Elliot, R. (1979), 'A Critical Evaluation of Fox's Radicalisation of Industrial Relations Theory', *Sociology*, January.

Wright, K. (1983), *Demarcation and Jurisdictional Disputes in Australia 1975−1979*, Industrial Relations Research Centre, University of New South Wales.

Wright, K. (1984), *Demarcation and Jurisdictional Disputes 1975−1979: Six Industry Case Studies*, Industrial Relations Research Centre, University of New South Wales.

Zeremes, M. (1985), *The Measurement of Earnings Drift*, Wages and Incomes Policy Research Paper No. 4, Department of Employment and Industrial Relations, Canberra.

Index